When the Water Calls...
We Follow

Thanks Mitch for helping us out, it was greatly appreciated

Jim Farris

When
The
Water Calls
We Follow

**Twenty-seven Different
Perspectives and Reflections
On Cruising the
Great Loop
Boating Adventure**

Edited by Jim & Lisa Favors

FAVORS VENTURES, LLC
Traverse City, Michigan

ISBN-10: 0-615-22161-0
ISBN-13: 978-0-615-22161-8

Published by:
Favors Ventures, LLC
P.O. Box 584
Traverse City, Michigan 49685

www.favorsventures.com
www.favorsgreatloopblog.com
www.favorsweb.com
www.womenonboardcruising.com
www.trailertrawlerlife.com

Cover and manuscript design by Design Favors – www.designfavors.net
Location photography by Lisa Targal Favors – www.stockfavors.com

Questions regarding the content or ordering of this book should be addressed to:
Favors Ventures, LLC
info@favorsventures.com

Printed in the United States of America

We dedicate this book to our three sons;
Bart, Skyler, and Ross,
whom we have encouraged, whether by word or example,
to always follow their dreams.

And the end of all our exploring
Will be to arrive where we started
And know the place for the first time.

-T.S. Eliot

CONTENTS

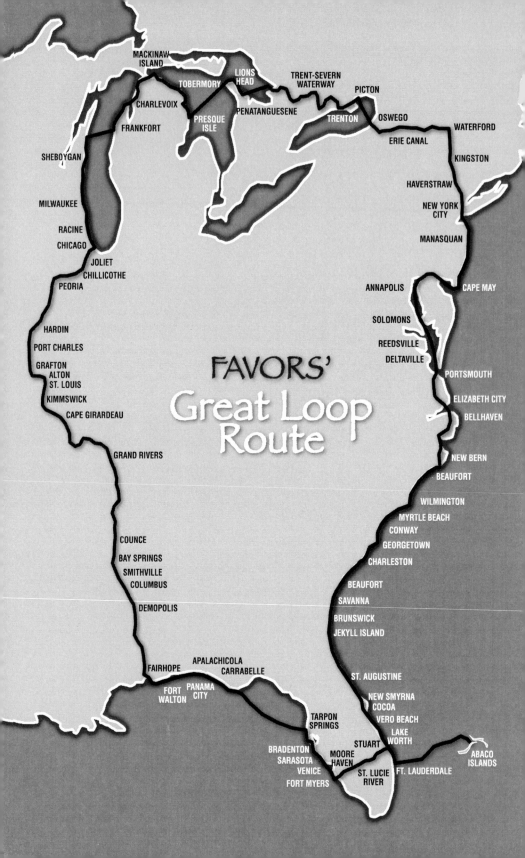

MACKINAW ISLAND

TOBERMORY

LIONS HEAD

TRENT-SEVERN WATERWAY

PICTON

CHARLEVOIX

PENATANGUESENE

PRESQUE ISLE

TRENTON

OSWEGO

WATERFORD

FRANKFORT

ERIE CANAL

KINGSTON

SHEBOYGAN

HAVERSTRAW

MILWAUKEE

NEW YORK CITY

RACINE

MANASQUAN

CHICAGO

JOLIET

CHILLICOTHE

PEORIA

ANNAPOLIS

CAPE MAY

SOLOMONS

HARDIN

REEDSVILLE

PORT CHARLES

DELTAVILLE

GRAFTON

ALTON

ST. LOUIS

PORTSMOUTH

KIMMSWICK

ELIZABETH CITY

CAPE GIRARDEAU

BELLHAVEN

FAVORS'

Great Loop Route

GRAND RIVERS

NEW BERN

BEAUFORT

WILMINGTON

MYRTLE BEACH

CONWAY

GEORGETOWN

COUNCE

CHARLESTON

BAY SPRINGS

SMITHVILLE

BEAUFORT

COLUMBUS

SAVANNA

DEMOPOLIS

BRUNSWICK

JEKYLL ISLAND

APALACHICOLA

CARRABELLE

ST. AUGUSTINE

FAIRHOPE

FORT WALTON

PANAMA CITY

NEW SMYRNA

COCOA

VERO BEACH

TARPON SPRINGS

LAKE WORTH

STUART

BRADENTON

SARASOTA

MOORE HAVEN

ABACO ISLANDS

VENICE

FORT MYERS

ST. LUCIE RIVER

FT. LAUDERDALE

FOREWORD

The idea for this book first came to us during the initial stages of our own Great Loop Adventure, somewhere around Tennessee. When we left our homeport of Charlevoix, Michigan, we only knew of one other couple who were soon to embark on the "Loop." So, while we had researched the route, got our boat "shipshape" and put our affairs in order, we had no real preconceived notions of what or whom we would encounter. We really didn't know what type of adventure, on the intangible side, we would actually end up experiencing.

What we found quite soon into our journey was that the American Great Loop travelers, more fondly known as "Loopers," were as varied as the members of any large family. As we met these fellow boaters, who, it became apparent, shared the same interests as us (boating and adventure), we realized that we had all left behind the self-importance of our home and working life. It didn't matter where we came from, where we worked or what our social, economic, or educational background was. We found that the camaraderie of this family was akin to belonging to a benevolent civic organization; all willing to help each other out without expecting anything in return.

With the revelation that there was more going on here than just a trip, route, or destination, and that maybe for many, like us, it was a life-changing experience; we got the idea for the book. We thought people would be interested in learning about the trials and tribulations such a trip affords its participants.

Our thoughts were to ask other boaters we met to share their varied and insightful experiences with us, while keeping their responses more philosophical in nature with little stories that were still fresh in their minds, ones that had made their trip valuable to them. As much as possible, we wanted to stay away from the cost of fuel, itineraries, and journal entries. We did this so you, the reader, could get a sense of what the Loopers experienced, how they overcame obstacles, what they enjoyed, how they got along with their "crew" for such a long time in a small space and, in a number of cases, how some Loopers accomplished the 6,000-mile trip mostly, or completely, by themselves. Even more importantly, we wanted to show why people left the comforts of home to tackle a trip like this, and what they ultimately gained.

We hoped to create a vehicle for people either considering this trip, or just curious about it, to have a better sense of what a journey like this can entail in an untouchable sense. In our opinion, the American Great Loop Adventure is more about the day-to-day journey, relationships, communing with nature, and most definitely not about the final destination or even the itinerary. If embarked upon, this trip would enhance and enrich the lives of anyone who has a taste for adventure, and a heart ripe for surprises, both large and small.

Charlevoix, Michigan

Lisa & Jim Favors - $\mathcal{K}$ISMET
Charlevoix, Michigan

Jim –

Lisa and I bought our first boat together within a year after we married. It was a second marriage for us both, and between us, we had Lisa's one son, Skyler, and my two sons, Bart and Ross. When we moved into our new (to us) family home, the boys wanted to get a dog and we agreed – as long as we could wait until springtime. As this time period approached, and the more we thought about this idea, the more we decided we really didn't want the added responsibility at that time. It's not that we don't like dogs; it was just that we were busy, with both of us working and the boys were in school and active themselves, so we didn't think we could devote enough time to train and properly take care of an animal. Instead, we decided, unbeknownst to the boys, to buy a used 24-foot Four Winns runabout. We agonized over how we would break this news to them. I had come across an iron Scottie dog cut out of metal and attached to a spike, at an antique store. I bought it thinking that this might be the way to break into the conversation about how we were now going to have a boat but no dog.

When the time came we gathered the boys up in our usual family meeting place, the living room, and explained to them that we had good news and bad news. We showed them the dog and said that this was the only one they would be getting, and that was the bad news. Needless to say, they were very disappointed. We then explained that the good news was that we had just bought a boat. This was the last time we ever heard about getting a dog – so began our family boating adventures.

As a side note, "Spike" has become an icon of sorts in our family's traditions and history of practical jokes. He often gets "stuck" in unusual places all over the neighborhood, and even found his way into someone's suitcase on a family vacation, and was proudly planted in the lawn of a cottage we once rented. He's even travelled on the boat with us. We fondly consider him a symbol of how our passion for boating began.

Fast forward 15 years and two more boat changes, and you'd find us departing Charlevoix, Michigan mid-September on our 42-foot Silverton Convertible that we had owned for five years. We purchased the Silverton with Great Lakes cruising in mind, not a 6,000-mile journey. Although the boat did a great job for us on the trip, I'd have to say that if we had known then what we know now about boats, we would have made a more practical choice, such as our current boat – a 40-foot Fathom, a fast expedition-style trawler. We are planning our second two-year Loop on this boat.

Before shoving away from the dock, we joined America's Great Loop Cruisers' Association (AGLCA – www.greatloop.org). Because of the recognition of the AGLCA burgee we flew, and the daily e-mail postings this organization provides, we soon found new comrades and a support group while underway. We soon discovered that our fellow members of AGLCA were more than willing to help one another; this made our trip a better overall experience. The association with AGLCA enabled us to more quickly form not only friendships but sometimes long-lasting relationships than we would have had we not been members.

It was a magical day on Lake Michigan when we started our trip. It was mid-September and most Loopers had already been through northern Michigan, as Lake Michigan has a bad reputation of being unpredictable after Labor Day. We had a string of Indian summer type days, when the water was as soft as silk, and the sky was as clear as vodka – the kind of days you dream about as a power boater. This fair weather continued as we crossed the big lake to Wisconsin, and hop-scotched our way down to Chicago, Illinois. While there, we got to experience the skyscrapers, old bridges, and downtown Chicago, by going up the Chicago River in our dinghy. We went into the lock, and up the river through downtown, and then all the way back to our dock in Burnham

Harbor. It was a great experience to see one of America's great cities from the vantage point of a 10-foot dinghy.

From there, our route was the normal path followed by most Loopers who can't get under the low bridges which stretch over the Chicago River. We traveled to the Cal-Sag Channel, just south of Chicago, and headed southwest to the Illinois River and eventually down the Mississippi River. Heading south/southwest on the Illinois River, we moved slowly, realizing that we weren't traveling on a super highway; this is nature's scenic route, and we felt that there would be many surprises for us on the river system if we lingered.

I'm only going to mention two memorable stops we made on the Illinois River. With five days on the river behind us, we were becoming comfortable with our new surroundings, and had been anchoring out quite a bit. On the sixth day, we arrived shortly before sunset at an anchorage at Bath Chute, just off a bend in the river. This spot was quiet, peaceful, and secluded in the early evening, but a bit after dark, shortly after we'd retired for the night, we started to see big spotlight rays dancing up and down the shoreline and through our boat. This went on for about 20 minutes or more, and eventually we started to hear the slowly increasing drone of large diesel engines. It was like a monster's heavy breathing, and it was steadily and slowly, getting closer. We weren't sure what to expect when it finally arrived, we were full of anticipation as we watched, waited, and listened. Finally, after what seemed to be almost an hour, two mammoth tugs, one after the other, with huge barges finally rounded the bend in the river. We were glad to be safely tucked up into the small side channel, and out of harm's way. If you've never traveled the rivers, this is just one example of the kind of surprising entertainment opportunities you might expect when you venture out of your comfort zone and open yourself up to the unknown.

Two days later, we arrived at the town of Hardin, Illinois, the other memorable stop where the highly heralded Riverdock Restaurant sits just off the banks of the river. We'd read that they had the best beef brisket and homemade pies anywhere on the river, and we felt we should stay a night and partake. As we were tying up to the dock, a red and blue helicopter maneuvered overhead and landed about a 100 feet from us. Three people got out, and after securing the chopper, they proceeded up to the restaurant. It's not every day you have a helicopter land that close to your boat.

We left *Kismet* to take a walk, not thinking any more about the helicopter, and on the way back, we decided to stop at the restaurant so we could find out how long they were open until, we didn't want to miss the brisket. As we entered the restaurant, a waitress was getting two fresh pies out of the pie case, and I said jokingly, "You're not going to eat both of those yourself are you?"

She said, "Oh no, these are for Mr. Busch." As in Auggie Busch of Anheiser Busch in St. Louis, Missouri. Apparently, he flies the short distance up to the Riverdock Restaurant a few times a month in his helicopter or float plane. I guess you'd call him a regular. We had dinner that night, and the beef brisket and pie were everything we were promised they'd be. This also began our quest to taste and learn about local cuisines as we arrived in new, to us, areas.

When we got to the Mississippi River, we immediately felt the strong pull of the river's famous current, and noticed how the character changed from the mild Illinois to the swift, swirling, and wide Mississippi. It's everything you'd think it would be, and more.

After an overnight stop in Alton, we were eager to finally make our way for a stopover at a Looper legend: Hoppie's Marina, Kimmswick, Missouri. Hoppie's is nothing more than several old barges fastened together along the west bank of the river. It's rustic but very functional, with lots of character. Currently run by Fern, Hoppie, and their daughter Debbie, Hoppie's has been in business since 1935, when Hoppie's father started the business. Besides the family's warm and unique personalities, the best part about this stop is the informational meeting Fern conducts at 4:30 p.m. most days. She gives everyone that attends an up-to-date discussion on the current conditions a boater will find while traveling south on the Mississippi. She tells everyone about silted in anchorages, and talks about the dangers of eddies (whirlpools), wing dams, river fog, and more. As most boaters will spend up to four more nights on the Mississippi, this informational session is both a must and a blessing, and will help you navigate this temperamental giant. If nothing else, Fern puts the fear of God into you so you don't take the Mississippi River for granted, or treat it as business as usual.

Most Loopers head south on the Mississippi River as far as Cairo, Illinois, and then navigate east up the Ohio River in order to reach the Tennessee River. We stayed for a week in the Kentucky Lakes area, and then continued on to the Tennessee River, where we stayed for a month at Grand Harbor Marina, on the Yellow River, just before the start of the Tennessee-Tombigbee Waterway.

Because we both were interested to learn more about our country's past we decided to incorporate several side trips into our Loop trip by either borrowing a marina loaner car, or renting one. We took a side trip to Memphis, Tennessee, where we visited a home used as an "underground railroad" before and during the civil war. This was a place where they kept slaves until they could arrange safe passage to the north. We were able to climb down into the cellar, which was used for shelter and to hide the slaves until passage to the north and freedom became available. That day Lisa and I learned a great deal about that terrible time in our country's history.

We also visited the National Civil Rights Museum in Memphis, which is located adjacent to the hotel where Martin Luther King was assassinated. After parking our car, we proceeded to the front door, went inside and waited at the reception desk, so we could pay the entrance fee. Nobody came so we called out for assistance and still no one came. We used the rest room facilities and started to wander around the museum store, calling out, but still no one came to help us. We waited for about 10 minutes and then decided to walk outside, that's when we noticed the museum hours posted on the front door stating that they were closed on Mondays. It appears that the door had never latched when they had closed up the prior day. We never did get a tour of the museum.

After our stay at Grand Harbor came to an end, we headed around the bend not far from the marina toward the Tennessee-Tombigbee Waterway which runs through Mississippi and Alabama, until it finally dumps out into Mobile Bay. This route cuts out several 100s of miles of the trip, therefore saving money and fuel; it also cuts down on a lot of barge and tugboat traffic, as well as reducing the intense navigational focus needed to dodge debris on the Mississippi River.

Because we had a powerboat that could go faster, we decided that once we reached Carrabelle, Florida, we'd head across the Gulf of Mexico to Tarpon Springs, Florida, instead of hugging the coastline of the Panhandle as many slower boats do. As this stretch is long – 200 miles, you need to not only watch your weather for a good opening, but you need to leave in the dark of early morning so you can arrive at your destination during daylight, mainly to make sure you avoid running into the thousands of crab pots along the west coast of Florida. It's also wise to go with at least one other boat; that day our caravan had three, all faster boats, but we had to wait for six days in Carrabelle before we had a proper weather window to make the crossing. We spent this time with four other Loopers, watching the weather, dining out, having cocktail parties, game nights, and even an early Christmas turkey dinner with all the fixings.

After spending a week (too short) in Tarpon Springs, we headed into the Intracoastal Waterway (ICW) of Florida and slowly traveled south towards Fort Myers, where we stayed at Fort Myers Yacht Basin Marina, located right downtown, for a month. We frequented the waterfront Farmer's Market to get fresh produce, and sometimes flowers and shellfish. From this location, we drove up to Sarasota to visit the Ringling Brother's Circus Museum. We even experienced a boat blow up with a big fireball raging along the gas dock. During our stay in Fort Myers, we had a few friends visit us from home. Also, since there were about 15 Looper boats in the area, we organized a big Looper cocktail party at our marina.

Our next jaunt was east through Lake Okeechobee, instead of going to the Keys, as most Loopers do. We were more interested in crossing the Gulf Stream to spend some time in the Abaco Islands in the Bahamas, where we stayed for the better part of three weeks. Going to the Abaco Islands on our own boat has been on our "Bucket List" for a long time.

The Abacos are about a 65-mile run from Palm Beach to the West End of the islands. This is a short run under proper conditions. We waited six days for the ideal weather window, and our trip was uneventful. In fact, it was one of those sunny days boaters live for. The waters calmed to a slow roll as we got closer to our destination.

The Abacos Islands immediately provided us with turquoise waters, sandy beaches, endless anchoring opportunities, and friendly people, all in a picture perfect setting. When we anchored out at one of the uninhabited islands, Great Sale Cay, on a clear night, and there was no artificial lighting within sight, we experienced a pitch-black sky with millions of sparkling stars as bright as you've ever seen. No lights from land or cities far away, only us, and this truly magnificent wonder of nature, for miles around.

We slowly worked our way to Hope Town after stopping at many of the islands in-between, or anchoring out under the stars. We enjoyed the leisurely island life, and wished we could have stayed longer. Our one prearranged meeting with friends from home came together right on schedule, with us arriving in Hope Town one day ahead of time.

From the Abacos, we traveled back to Florida and then up the East Coast into Georgia and the Carolinas. We enjoyed the slow pace of life in all the small ICW communities where we stopped. These coastal towns have so much history, it's hard at times to believe we were traveling the same waters as Christopher Columbus once had.

It was on the East Coast that we had two separate, week-long visits from our sons, Ross and Skyler. First, Ross was able to join us in Beaufort, South Carolina for the portion of our trip from Beaufort to Charleston, South Carolina. He experienced a little of our Looping lifestyle, met some of our new friends, did some sightseeing with us in Charleston, and helped us close out the night in a weedy anchorage off of the ICW. We've often wondered if maybe we've had a little influence on him, as it relates to his own adventurous inclinations.

The only trip we made back to Michigan in nine-and-a-half months was to attend Skyler's graduation ceremony from Kendall College of Art and Design in Grand Rapids, Michigan. After the big day, Skyler rode back with us to New Bern, North Carolina, where *Kismet* was safely tied up to the dock of our new Looper friends, Wade and Susie's home which is just off the Neuse River. Then, with Skyler aboard, we traveled up to and through the Dismal Swamp Canal. He learned to negotiate locks, as well as spend time with us anchoring and touring Norfolk, Virginia before his return to Michigan and his quest for a full-time, post-college employment. It was great to have had this time to spend with family, and I think both Skyler and Ross felt the same way.

From Norfolk, we meandered up through the Chesapeake Bay to visit a few of the quaint towns we'd heard about, including Reedsville, Virginia, where we learned a great deal about the popular soft shell crabs from a local "crabber guy." We saw the tanks where they keep the crabs until they molt, and become "soft."

As our journey continued, we made our way up the New Jersey Coast to New York City. As we approached Sandy Hook, New Jersey, we could start to see the skyline of New York City begin to materialize in the distance. What a sight to see; one of the world's great cities, from the vantage point of our own boat. We were traveling the same water route taken by most of our ancestors as they arrived by boat to Ellis Island. After a slow tour of the harbor, we proceeded to an anchorage just behind the Statue of Liberty.

This was an incredibly memorable night in that we were anchoring within a short distance of one of the world's great landmarks. As night progressed, we were able to see the glow of the torch just above the trees in the nearby park, shivers ran up our spines as we pondered all that Lady Liberty stands for.

After three-day's of sightseeing in New York City, we headed up the Hudson River, towards the Erie Canal, where we entered another lock system; the same system used as the main transportation route to move cargo and people before trains, planes, and semi-trucks. The Erie and Oswego Canals delivered us to Lake Ontario, where we crossed over and into Canada. There, we took the Trent-Severn Waterway – another landmark, navigational route that traverses northwest through Ontario, ending at the base of the Georgian Bay.

The variety of experience and education that this trip brought us throughout the 6,000-mile journey was appreciated for what each area had to offer, and the lock system and small towns throughout the Erie Canal and Trent-Severn Waterway was no different. We could have spent a lot more time on both systems, however, time was marching on and we needed to return to our homeport and family. We loved our time here, however, our regret was not having enough time left to do more exploring. At this point, we were kind of like the horses you rent on Mackinaw Island; moving slowly and kind of meandering on the trail until reaching the turnaround path where thoughts of home loomed large on the horizon, our pace quickened as the lure and warmth of family and friends called to us.

We by-passed Georgian Bay and North Channel of Canada, as this is in our own back yard and we had already been there several times. However, for anyone on the Loop, we would encourage you to spend as much time as you can in this pristine area. It just doesn't get much better than this.

Our friends fell into two categories as it relates to how they felt about us leaving on this trip. There were those people that thought the Loop trip was a great adventure, and hoped to do the same or something like it themselves at some time in the future, and those that were polite to us but secretly thought we were absolutely out of our minds. Most of the second group, although great friends and nice people, are maybe not the adventuress type and would find it difficult to detour from life's normal routine.

Our non-boating friends and family, (and even some of our boating friends) would ask, "Do you find that you have enough room on your boat for such a long trip?" or, "Doesn't the boat get extremely small for two people?" We were asked this question in a variety of ways, and it finally dawned on us what they were really asking. They really wanted to know if the boat was big enough for the two of us.

Lisa and I both love boating, so we never gave any thought to existing in the full-time, close confines, of our 42-foot boat. A couple of weeks into the trip though, we had a little bit of a breakdown and had to have one of those discussions that guys just love to have with their wives. We figured out that we both needed to have some occasional alone time. We accomplished this by doing little things, such as going ashore to take showers at different times, not always running errands together, etc. Once we figured this out, we were fine, and the boat seemed bigger than it actually was.

When we left Charlevoix, Michigan, I can honestly say that I felt the trip would be a great way to explore and learn about our country. In the end, I'd say we were able to see more beauty in nature than I thought we would have, and that we experienced more friendship and kindness from all the people we met along the way, both Loopers and non-Loopers alike.

We felt lucky to be able to view the grandeur of the Sleeping Bear Sand Dunes from the waters of Lake Michigan, and enjoy the striking beauty of the skylines of Chicago and New York City, when you approach big harbors such as these by water; you are seeing these areas as most never do. We were also fortunate to: tour Forest Park in St. Louis, Missouri site of the 1904 Worlds Fair; enjoy the company of Fern and Hoppie at Hoppie's on the Mississippi River (a Looper tradition); have a family-style, sit down, catfish dinner at Bobby's Fish Camp (another Looper tradition) with a roomful of new Looper acquaintances. We also enjoyed visiting the many museums, battlefields and ships; talk with the colorful tug boat captains on the radio; anchor out in the quiet glory of Mother Nature; experience the current of the rivers; put together several impromptu potluck dinners, or cocktail parties; anchor behind the Statue of Liberty on our own boat, view the skyline of New York City; and to cross the Gulf Stream to the Abaco Islands. When, as a boater, you are able to do some of these trips, I feel you have lived a richer life.

The biggest benefit of the trip was never on the radar screen at the onset. The real bonus we received from leaving home, friends, and family for nine-and-a-half months was all the new friends we made among our fellow Loopers.

The other part of this equation involved the people who lived in all of the waterfront towns we visited. With rare exception, the people we met along the way were kind, courteous, willing to help, give guidance or assistance, some would even lend us their car or give us a lift to the local market. We hadn't thought too much about this aspect of our adventure beforehand, and therefore it was both a wonderful surprise and gave us a great deal of respect and a sense of pride in the fiber of America.

We wanted to experience the Great Loop because we love everything about boating (except the price of fuel), we felt the 6,000-mile journey would be an adventure that the two of us could experience together doing what we both love. The trip gave us an opportunity to learn more about our country, meet many interesting, like-minded people, and see places we'd most likely never see unless we were traveling by boat.

Life's too short!

We took the trip because we are in good health, we felt we could afford the expense, and we were excited about the prospect of an adventure. Most importantly, I had come to a point in my life where I no longer felt like I would live forever, and I think this happens to all of us at some point: we realize we are mortal. For me, the realization hit home because of the deaths of people I knew (most my age). These reasons, and other unfortunate life-changing events to people we know, also world events during the years leading up to when we made our decision to retire and do the Great Loop, convinced us to stop and take stock of our lives. We decided to simplify our lifestyle and focus on what we enjoy doing, and not what we had to do in life to get by.

We are in a unique situation at this stage of our lives in that our children are independent and living on their own, and our parents are in reasonably good health for their ages, as well as being independent. Because of this, we felt comfortable leaving the security of our comfort zone for a nine-and-a-half-month boat trip, the length of time we took to do the Loop – which in hindsight, is not nearly long enough. Our family members were understanding and supportive of our decision to leave on this trip. We made a completely clean break, we sold our family home, sold a lot of "stuff," put everything in storage and left on the Great Loop. This added freedom enabled us to maintain our focus on the Loop trip, so we could get the most out of the experience.

Lisa –

Fifteen years ago, a short time before he proposed to me, Jim made a promise to me, "I'll take you places you've never been before." As a young woman, I had traveled to Europe with family a few times and once by myself. I had always yearned for more travel adventures, so the prospect of being with the man I loved while exploring unknown places certainly intrigued me. If a marriage can have a theme to it, ours would be the continual quest to broaden our horizons. Jim has tried his best to find places to show me that I've never seen before. It may just be a road off the beaten path in our hometown, or something as immense as the bottom of the Grand Canyon. In our effort to see and experience new and interesting places, we have discovered what the real meaning of "home" is, and we revel in the knowledge that we are truly at home when we are with our family and/or each other... no matter where that happens to be.

One summer, a few years before we retired, while out in our dinghy, in our homeport of Charlevoix, Michigan, we saw the boat *Bacaruda* anchored out in Round Lake. On the transom, it said: Seattle, Washington, we were intrigued. What would it be like to travel from the West Coast, through the Panama Canal all the way up to the Great Lakes? Because our interest was piqued, we decided to introduce ourselves and learn as much as we could about the particulars of such a trip. After a brief introduction, we invited the Miller's for cocktails on our boat later that evening, they accepted and the rest is history, as they say, because that chance encounter changed our lives forever. Who knows, we may have still gotten to the same spot eventually but maybe not. We think that it truly was... *Kismet*.

The Millers were very helpful in answering all of our questions about traveling long distance by boat. What we were surprised to learn though, was that even a boat their size (48 feet) could make a journey around the eastern United States on a circular route, which after cruising the West Coast, the Panama Canal, and the Caribbean, was the route of their current voyage. This trip is sometimes called the Circle Route but more often than not it's referred to as the Great Loop.

While we had become avid boaters during our marriage we were not aware that pleasure craft could do this trip as easily as they were telling us. From that moment on, we were obsessed about retiring early, we began planning so that we could experience this adventure ourselves. We were first surprised, and then happy that we were both in total agreement about focusing our energies toward one goal – becoming Loopers.

I had recently retired, and Jim was thinking about retiring in a few years when we met the Millers. The idea of doing the Loop made us step up the thinking and planning and about three years later, we started to put the plan in motion. We put our house up for sale, instead of renting it out or closing it up, so that we wouldn't have to worry about anything while we were gone. It turned out that selling was the right thing, since we were totally worry-free during our trip, and we had sold at the height of the market - one month before we left on our trip - just before the real estate market plummeted in Michigan.

As "D" (departure) day approached, we went through our home and purged as much as we could, knowing that what was left was going into storage in the near future. We made every doctor appointment we thought necessary, and had all the recommended tests taken, we also acquired enough refills of one or two prescriptions we needed to have. Jim arranged to have our mail sent to us at designated spots where we stayed a week or more. Mail day was always fun because we had a big pile of surprises to go through - we thought it funny - the importance mail day played in our new lives. (There was always a hope for news from home or just an anticipated magazine, even catalogs were a welcome diversion from boat chores.) We did a lot of maintenance and repairs on the boat, to get her into shape so that we wouldn't have any immediate surprises. We arranged to pay for most of our bills online, and I put together a list of what we thought would be essentials for the trip.

We joined America's Great Loop Cruisers' Association (AGLCA) and did as much research as we could on anchorages and places to visit along the route. The summer before we left, we tried to get as much first-hand knowledge as we could from all the Loopers who came through Charlevoix. In all the time we planned, we never had a moment's hesitation as to whether this was the right thing to do. We were both "on board" 100%.

On September 15, we left our homeport of Charlevoix, Michigan, to experience an adventure of a lifetime.

There was an enormous rush of excitement, openness, and curiosity about the unknown when we pushed away from our dock. Since we departed near the tail-end of the summer season, we didn't meet up with any other Loopers until we reached Chicago, Illinois. The further south we got, the more opportunity there was to meet and socialize with others that were "just like us." I think this is one of the interesting things about a trip like this - it's the chance to meet people who are "in the same boat" as us. We are all cruising around this circle route on boats, seeking adventure, braving the unknown, sharing companionship and camaraderie, while at the same time facing the possibility of calamity around every bend in a river or over the next open body of water. The other Loopers we met became the highlight of our trip. In fact, when we see or hear comments people make about their experiences while on the Loop, invariably, the first thing they go on and on about are the people they've met. Friendships have endured way beyond the adventure itself, as we now know from personal experience. I guess you could look at it as if it was a living, growing reminder of the experience, friendships do indeed flourish even after crossing one's wake.

We didn't have much company with us on the trip except a few friends who stayed a night each while we were at marinas. As Jim mentioned earlier, two of our sons, Ross and Skyler, came at different times, and each spent a week with us. These two visits were another high point for us since we could actually share a little of our trip with them, and they could understand a little more about what we were off doing when they didn't see us for long periods of time.

We came to feel that our boat was just right for the two of us to be comfortable, so we didn't invite guests other than our sons to actually travel with us. It was the right decision for us because of the accommodations on the boat. We have just recently moved aboard our new *Kismet*, a Fathom 40, which has more interior room, we are hoping all three of our sons will join us again and both of our mother's as well.

We talked to many people who traveled with company almost the whole trip. One Looper boat consisted of two couples that we think managed to complete the trip together. Numerous boaters had grandchildren meet them for extended periods, in areas that they thought would be interesting or educational for the children. We were continually surprised at the variety of ways people socialized while on this trip.

Our family and friends were supportive about our adventure, and many followed our website and blog to see where we were and what we were doing. Our boys weren't surprised by our decision to do this trip since they know how nuts we are about boating. If we worried about family, it was more for our parents since we wouldn't have the close contact with them that we usually enjoyed. Our friends were supportive, and asked many questions about how this would work. While no one other than our sons joined us on board during our first trip, quite a few did meet up with us while on their vacations, or we met them in their hometowns in Chicago, Florida, the Abacos, New Jersey, and New York City.

People asked us, "Did the boat get a little small?" It was their way of asking if we got along in the confines of the boat. Well, I can't honestly say that it was a piece of cake all the time, but after the first month and a half, we finally worked out some issues of space and togetherness. I guess we looked at it as a small hurdle in front of something even greater, and since this trip was so desired by both of us, we made a real effort to adjust.

Since I had retired a few years before Jim, I had acquired a daily routine of working at home by myself. I was used to having my own schedule. I did all the shopping alone, and when I worked on chores, projects etc. I enjoyed the quiet without interruptions in my routine. I think it is the typical situation where one partner, who was working full time, suddenly is home 24/7 with the other who already has an established regimen. The sudden togetherness of retirement can be an adjustment for two adults, only for us, we also found ourselves making this adjustment on a 42-foot boat.

When Jim retired, at the beginning of the summer before we left, we were so busy selling the house, moving, provisioning the boat, and putting our affairs in order that daily life together while traveling on a boat didn't hit us for a couple of weeks into our trip. Suddenly, we were doing EVERYTHING together; even the little things like shopping. I wasn't used to so much togetherness and didn't think it would be healthy for us. Therefore, we had to make time to talk about our individual frustrations and needs, which are each different from the other's. We had to acknowledge and respect those differences. We figured out a way to be more aware of the other's desires and personalities. We had to compromise so that we could both be happy and thrive. During the trip, we learned a lot about each other that we hadn't known before.

People also asked, "What do you do all day on the boat?" I'm sure it's different for everyone. I took projects and brought books and manuals to further my education on web design and video production. I maintained a blog site for our family and friends to keep track of us. I honed up on my photography skills to thoroughly document our trip. I like to cook so we have a well-stocked kitchen as far as equipment, etc. I enjoyed trying my hand at the current local dishes; collecting recipes of dishes we had never heard of or tried before. It all kept me busy so that I was truly never bored. Jim read voraciously, and developed a keen interest in planning our sightseeing trips, from borrowing or renting cars to visiting historical landmarks or art museums. We both loved trying local cuisines in tiny or obscure restaurants, this led to many memorable meals in out of the way places.

While we did have an adjustment to make in the lifestyle we found ourselves sharing, I have to say that I can't think of anyone else with whom I would want to share an adventure like this. With Jim's energy, sunny disposition, eagerness to please, and competence as a captain and mechanic, I always felt fortunate that I had such a loving, outgoing partner to share this incredible experience with.

I don't recall any worst experiences while on the trip. We didn't have any boating or major health disasters so we lucked out there. I guess the hardest time for me was when, in the Abacos, I learned from an e-mail that my youngest brother Mart, who lives in Florida, had just had a heart attack. The frustrating part was trying to get in contact with my family while we were on an island with a complicated phone card system. We walked to the top of the hill on Green Turtle Cay Island, where there was reported to be a pay phone, but we couldn't get it to work. Our cell didn't work in the Bahamas, and e-mail was sporadic at best. I desperately wanted to talk to someone in our family and be reassured that he was OK. We did finally connect with him by a phone we found in a nearby hotel on the Grand Bahama Island, just before we headed back to the States.

I do remember having apprehensions, and feeling worried about impending disasters just before approaching the Mississippi River with its floating debris, intense current and whirlpools; while waiting to cross the Gulf of Mexico; and the whole week prior to navigating to the Bahamas through the Gulf Stream. I dreamt of huge tsunami waves and of *Kismet* trying to stay afloat, or plunging bow first into the bottom of the dark, swirling waters. We were extremely careful though; we waited for ideal weather conditions during those anxious times and it always paid off.

Like many other Loopers, as far as best experiences, I would have to say that there have been many, such as meeting all the other adventurous boaters along the way, and hearing their stories and circumstances. Crossing from Florida through the Gulf Stream to the Abaco Islands was a real thrill. The opportunity to approach New York City and the Statue of Liberty by our own boat, and being able to anchor right behind "Lady Liberty" for the night was exhilarating. Cruising on the Trent-Severn Waterway has always been a dream of ours and we weren't disappointed.

Looking back I find that most of my fondest memories include people. We found that whenever Loopers bunched up at a marina, cocktails emerged, or a potluck was planned with amazing food being created from all the little kitchens aboard the Looper boats. During these get-togethers, contacts were made and boat cards exchanged, along with stories of each other's experiences along the route. Sometimes, the navigators met to compare charts, routes and share knowledge. Often, it meant meeting up with someone you met earlier, and catching up on where they went and what they saw, and sometimes what we missed.

I also remember the many colorful tug/tow operators on the river system. They have their own language, and if you treat them courteously, they will return the favor. We heard stories of people who disregarded their position on the rivers, and paid dearly for it later on down river because word about inconsiderate recreational boaters gets passed along from one tug to another. It was hard to understand them sometimes, with their unfamiliar accents and protocol, but if you show them the respect they deserve they'll go out of their way to let you pass when needed or they'll even give helpful instructions to help you get past them, or they may hold back so you can catch the lock ahead of them.

The lock masters were also a treat. You can spend a lot of time tied up in a lock, and occasionally you will get a chatty lock master. You can garner needed information this way about an unfamiliar territory, local politics and occasionally an insight into a pretty unconventional job situation. There were times, transiting locks, where we never saw a person or a face, maybe just heard a voice from a loud speaker giving us instructions for locking through. That was always kind of eerie especially in some of the bigger locks where the hidden voice would echo off the lock chamber walls. Once in a while a lock master could get pretty irate with the captains of some boats who didn't get the process and combine that frustration with the loud speaker situation and you have some pretty entertaining dialog – except this performance was only humorous until your time came to enter the lock.

In the Abacos, we listened to the daily radio program, Cruiser's Net, which airs at 8:15 a.m. every morning on VHF 68, delivering the local news, messages between people, and weather reports. It seemed to shorten the distance between the islands and people. I remember while we were there, a young man had taken off in a family member's boat and hadn't been seen for several days. This was the hot topic during our stay, and as I remember, the story had a happy ending.

Jim & Lisa Favors - *Kismet*

We met many local townspeople along the way; some were curious as to what we were doing, many offered help or guidance while in their area. These encounters were precious to us as it warmed our hearts to meet people so open, friendly, and eager to help.

I have to say that Jim really outdid himself this time in his quest to impress me with new horizons. I will never forget the anticipation of arriving at and exploring new (to us) territory. We did a lot of celebrating on the back deck after reaching certain milestones of the trip. There were many, and they were savored thoroughly by us simply because we did this together.

In hindsight, I think what we did, by taking this trip, was that we left our comfort zone, our house, our family, and friends, for a chance at adventure. In return, we have gained something we never would have otherwise – confidence in our instincts, the ability to think creatively about our lives, and the opportunity to widen our perspective of the world and the people in it. In the end, I think, as we look back, it seems that the more we venture out to wander and explore, the bigger the world and opportunities for exploration become. When we retired and took the "plunge," our lives changed forever. We are now more open to spontaneous pursuits and unknown avenues than we ever were before, when we were raising a family. The horizon in our lives has changed dramatically.

We never expected or planned to be doing this. We would have been happy, before we knew about the Loop, to just be cruising in the confines of our beautiful Great Lakes, living on our boat during the summer season. Now, we wonder where our next trip will lead us, because we can't possibly know. We have put a road map to our remaining, active years, and right now, we are traveling on it however we can. We know that in the future, we'll have to settle down again when age or health dictates, but in the meantime, we are on a mission to be open to explore.

We were lucky in that although Jim and I are, quite often, complete opposites, we always seem to be on the same page when it comes to planning our lives and the adventures we seek. I think we are both so thankful to have the support and energy of each other when planning and experiencing something new, because while opportunities for adventure are so much a part of our individual lives, I don't think either one of us would enjoy doing any of this without the other.

Chicago, Illinois

Christopher Shustak - *Aanoosh*
Jamestown, Rhode Island

For most people, the decision to set off on a multi-year sailing adventure stands upon years of careful research, planning, and preparation. They work their way through the classes at the local Power Squadron, get 100s of hours of experience on the boat that they hope to take to sea, and jump on every opportunity to pick the brains of anyone who looks remotely salty at the local West Marine store. In my case, it was much more of a snap decision. It took just about a year to transition from a dirt-dwelling existence, where I didn't own a boat, to actually living aboard a peripatetic cruising vessel. Although I had extensive experience sailing small boats, and had completed a Coast Guard Better Boating and Seamanship class 25 years before, I had never sailed anything larger than a 16-foot daysailor. I couldn't read a navigational chart, and had never dropped an anchor beyond burying one in the sand when I pulled my daysailor up onto the beach for an afternoon picnic.

Well, I'm not being entirely truthful. The idea for a sailing voyage had been percolating in the back of my mind since I was old enough to crawl. My dad and my uncle had always loved boats, so dozens of maritime books graced the shelves in our basement library. We spent most family vacations on Nantucket (before it turned into the uber-priced playground of the rich and famous), and I can remember countless walks along the docks looking at boats, talking to skippers and fishermen, and taking in the sights, sounds, and smells of the waterfront. This environment was part and parcel of the Nantucket cultural experience, dating back to the days when whaling ships and clippers roamed the oceans. I remember that my uncle had spoken many times of his plan to build a boat that could serve as the basis for an Intracoastal cruising adventure, and he actually obtained a set of plans that would produce a vessel worthy of the trip. As a result, this sort of environment provided the necessary catalyst that enticed me to purchase a copy of Robin Lee Graham's book *Dove* when I stumbled upon it at a junior high school book fair.

Even though the book was filled with lurid accounts of rough seas, storms, treacherous coral reefs and deadly sea creatures, I never remember being scared of the idea of setting forth on a similar journey. I only remember thinking about the challenge, the opportunities to prove self-sufficiency, and the chance to see parts of the world that were so very different from my monotonous, white, middle-class town in New England. I remember promising myself that I would someday set off on a similar adventure, and I spent many hours in study hall thinking about how I'd pull it off, while reading book after book about boats, cruising, and sailing.

As enthusiastic as I was about the idea, however, I never actually got around to making this dream a reality. After graduating from high school and earning a bachelors degree from a slightly snooty liberal arts college, I settled into a series of exploratory jobs that finally led me into starting a computer-consulting firm in the early nineties. Life then settled into a fairly lucrative routine that varied little over the next 14 years. I frequently thought about my dream, but always found excuses why it wasn't the right time. I convinced myself that too many customers relied upon my services to allow me to spend so much time away. My elderly aunt needed someone to cut grass and shovel snow. I had three dogs that required daily walks, grooming, and gourmet food. I couldn't just relinquish my responsibilities while spending time and money on a "dream." Besides, what was the rush? I had decades ahead of me to spend on leisure activities. Now was the time to work.

Sometime in the fall of 2003, a close friend, who was two years younger than me, had a massive heart attack, and nearly dropped dead in the parking garage at work. Doctors at the hospital discovered that four of his coronary arteries were blocked, and rushed him to the OR for an emergency angioplasty. Visiting him at the hospital, I couldn't shake a disturbing vision. I clearly visualized myself lying in that hospital bed. My friend and I were both similar in age, and we both took pretty decent care of ourselves. We both exercised, didn't use drugs or tobacco, and typically followed a pretty healthy diet. This vision was no fantasy. I had already reached the age where illnesses were claiming members of my peer group, and here was my best friend, lying in a bed, having barely escaped a date with the Grim Reaper.

Thoroughly shaken, I left the hospital, and stopped in to see my 83-year-old aunt – the one who had married my boat-loving uncle. I confided in her that my friend's illness had destroyed my sense of complacency, and told her about the boat trip. I asked her if I was crazy to consider such a disruptive plan, and asked her for advice. Pouring a cup of tea, she related that my uncle kept the boat plans that he purchased in the top drawer of his desk. Every week, he'd thumb through the folder, and would dream about the Intracoastal Waterway, the ports of call along the way, and an ultimate landfall at Key West. Invariably, he'd close the folder, and return it to the drawer. He always chose to follow the path of responsibility, safety and comfort. He continued to go to his job, to shovel the snow, and to cut the grass.

After retirement, diabetes, gout, and old age weakened his balance, strength, and stamina. He no longer had the ability to build his boat, nor to complete the voyage. My aunt told me that not a day went by during those twilight years where he didn't regret his decision to postpone the trip. He died, never having taken one step toward his dream.

"You have the ability to ensure that my Harry didn't die in vain," she said. "You can always find a job, or start another business. You can always find that gentleman's farm complete with Belgian draft horses and Jersey cows. You can always get married to the right girl, and settle down. You can't always go sailing. Buy the boat. Stop wasting an opportunity that may never come around again. You don't want to be sitting in a wheelchair with a lap full of regrets." She was right. By the time I made it home that night, I made the decision to buy a boat, shut down my business, and head to sea.

Most friends had other ideas. They thought me crazy for abandoning the safety and reliability of a conventional middle-aged lifestyle. "How could you give up a decent career?" they asked. "Leaving friends and family for an undetermined length of time?" Wasn't I being completely irresponsible to chase after a dream? A few of them were actually scared for my safety. I later learned that they debated among themselves whether I'd be drowned in a storm, disappear in the Bermuda triangle, shot by pirates, or run down by a rogue freighter. For some reason, I never took any of them seriously, and never gave much thought to any of the negatives associated with the idea. Thousands of people took to the oceans, some navigating through the Loop, and some gunk holing through the Bahamas. Others drifted through the Caribbean, while the rest circumnavigated the globe. Very few of them came to serious harm. I figured if I applied common sense, and didn't take too many unnecessary chances, I'd likely emerge from the experience slightly bloodied but alive, and at the same time more experienced, skilled, and mature.

It took about a year to locate a suitable boat, but after an organized search using the telephone, magazine advertisements, and Internet postings, I ended up finding a 40-foot Pacific Seacraft cutter-rigged sailboat berthed on the West Coast of Florida. I can't say that a blue-water sailboat would be anyone's first choice for a Great Loop trip, but she served me well over the entire journey. The boat sported two sleeping cabins, a head with a separate shower stall, and a decent-sized galley with gas stove and oven, and a refrigerator/freezer. A settee lay in front of the galley area that would easily seat six, and a very nice nav station had been installed on the opposing side.

The crew that finally set sail with me ended up having four legs instead of two. I had initially planned to do the trip with my girlfriend, but those plans fell through very close to our departure date. I couldn't find anyone to pet sit my animals, so they came along for the ride. I tried to convince the dogs and cat to stand watch, trim sails, and handle dock lines, but they continually refused to cooperate - something about these activities not being part of the union contract. As a result, I single-handed the vessel throughout the entire voyage.

Single-handing a 40-foot boat isn't easy. It's often exhausting, frustrating, and scary. There is no one to steer the boat while consulting charts. There is no co-captain to ask for advice in an emergency, and no one to hold a light when cleaning weeds out of the engine cooling system. Even so, there were significant advantages. Single-handed sailing provided an almost unlimited opportunity to develop my problem solving skills, confidence in my capabilities, and increased self-esteem. It demonstrated that I possessed the ability to think clearly under pressure, and forced me to learn to function effectively even though my body was wracked with fear, fatigue, and discomfort.

Most people with whom I've chatted often ask if I was ever lonely during my trip. I can't remember a single occasion where I missed companionship. First, I shared the boat with three dogs and a cat, all of which snoozed in the cockpit in good weather, but took refuge under the settee table in bad. Second, most anchorages and marinas were populated with boats that were filled with friendly, interesting, and outgoing people. Almost every evening was filled with a cocktail or two (never more), dinner on someone's boat, and stimulating conversation afterwards.

Finally, there were so many things that demanded my attention on the boat (maintenance, cleaning, cooking, laundry, and chart plotting to state a few) that I had no time to be lonely. While underway, I had the ham radio, the VHF marine, and a marine SSB to reach other boaters, and could always find adventurous soul mates who wished to visit a shore side watering hole for a beer at the end of the day, or would be willing to head off to the favorite snorkeling spot for a morning swim. In the few instances where I did have free time, I read the 15 cases of books that passed through my library at various times during the trip. Looking back on it, my social life aboard actually ended up being considerably more active than the one that I had left back home.

My trip officially began in Naples, Florida, where the previous owner owned a vacation home. I moved aboard the boat early in the winter and spent a number of weeks updating equipment, and maintaining various systems on the boat. The broker offered very little assistance beyond the initial sale, so there was a steep learning curve as I tried to decipher how to change engine oil, configure the electronics, and operate the holding tank/head setup. Thank goodness, Pacific Seacraft was only a phone call away, and the company officials were more than willing to answer the myriad of questions that popped up during this period.

When I departed Fort Myers in February, I really didn't have a firm plan in place. I knew that a circumnavigation would be a bit of a stretch considering my level of expertise, and my choice of crew. Instead, I assembled a list of possible destinations loosely associated with a Great Loop trip. These included The Dry Tortugas, the Intracoastal Waterway, Bermuda, the Bahamas, the Great Lakes, the North Channel, and the coast of Maine and the Atlantic Maritimes. I even included the idea of a Caribbean trip or crossing the Atlantic via Bermuda, the Azores, and Gibraltar. If some part of the trip proved unreasonable, I'd alter my plans accordingly.

I ended up following the Great Loop route from Fort Myers south around Key West, and then northward, paralleling the East Coast via the

Chesapeake, the Delaware Bay, and the Hudson River. Pulling my mast in Catskill, New York, I entered the Erie Canal, heading west across New York State. Canadian officials counseled against trying to navigate the Trent-Severn with a draft greater than five feet, so I continued along the Erie to Tonawanda, restepped the mast at Wardells, and sailed through Lake Erie, Lake Huron, and Lake Michigan to Chicago. From there, I restowed my mast on deck, and headed down the inland river system to Mobile, Alabama. From that point, I hugged the West Coast of Florida, and finally tied my Loop once I reached Fort Myers. I then bisected Florida on the Okeechobee Canal to spend the winter in the Bahamas. Reaching Georgetown at the southwest end of the Bahamian archipelago, I jettisoned plans to head to the Caribbean and South America for the hurricane season, on account of lousy sailing weather heading southeast. Instead, I backtracked, heading north to Marsh Harbor, where I then departed on an eight-day crossing to Bermuda. After staying there for three weeks, I sailed from St. George's Harbor Bermuda to Newport Rhode Island, and spent the summer and fall cruising along the Maine coast. The entire adventure took a little less than two years.

I'm not exaggerating when I say that I truly enjoyed every part of the trip. I fondly remember the stunning sunsets on the Gulf of Mexico and the Bahama Bank, as well as the pine-scented anchorages on Casco Bay. The sight of the Statue of Liberty as I entered New York Harbor literally took my breath away, and the New Year's Eve fireworks seen from the Vinoy Bay anchorage in St. Petersburg Florida were better than any shore-side party. As wonderful as all of these experiences proved to be, there was one experience that I'll never forget – the first night of my bluewater passage to Bermuda. Once land faded from sight, and the sun set for the day, the night sky revealed a stunning collage of constellations spread across the blackened heavens – a canvas that was completely free from the glare of city lights. Words cannot describe the peaceful beauty of the following morning as the sun poked above the horizon on a completely empty ocean. I took great satisfaction from completing the Great Loop trip, but nothing compared to the triumph of pulling into St. George's Harbor Bermuda after an eight-day, single-handed passage.

Things weren't always so sanguine. There were many times where I was queasy enough that I skipped eating for 24 hours at a time. November temperatures in Alabama often dropped below freezing, and I often shivered during some of those long, cold nights. I came across a small number of unpleasant people operating some of the marinas, a few of the drawbridges in Florida, and the locks along the Illinois River. Even so, I can't forget the kindness, hospitality and generosity shown by the great majority of the people who I came across. Too many people fed me dinner when I was exhausted after a long day on the water, lent me cars so that I could restock the boat from the nearby supermarket, or helped me repair things that would cost hundreds of dollars if I hired someone from a nearby boat yard. The only thing they ever asked in return was a promise that I would extend the same courtesy when I came across a fellow boater in need. Not once did I ever fail to deliver on that pledge.

I'll never claim that cruising on a small boat is easy. It's often uncomfortable, frustrating, risky, and expensive. Periods of comfortable routine can instantly transform into heart-stopping chaos. Regardless, I consider my boat trip to be one of the most rewarding and valuable experiences in my entire life. I learned more about people, my country, and my own self in two years than I had learned in the previous 40, and although my decision to set sail involved considerable sacrifice, I'd make the same choice in a second.

If you've ever thought about taking a similar step, put your fears aside and take the plunge. I guarantee that when you return, you'll conclude that you made the right choice. I certainly did.

St. Louis, Missouri

Sue & John Winter - *Miss* LIBERTY
Charlotte, North Carolina

We started our Loop in Wilmington, North Carolina, heading north from the Wilmington Marine Center. We decided to leave in April, before most Loopers usually depart from this area, because we wanted to travel a few more miles so that we could see the Long Island Sound, Outer Banks, Lake Champlain, and the Rideau Canal. We planned to take at least one year; depending on what side trips we took, such as the Bahamas. We estimate that we will travel about 7,000 miles minimum. We are doing it continuously, until we complete it, with three, week-long trips planned to visit home to get our grandkid fixes, as they are growing fast at ages five and six years. It also allows us to plan between legs of the trip and coordinate easier connections for friends/family who want to join us. This worked out well for us.

Our vessel is a Cruisers 39 with a flybridge, two staterooms, and almost all the amenities we needed for living on a boat. We have gas engines, which we have calculated is cheaper than the diesel, which most prefer. The size is great for anchoring and it's easier finding a marina to accommodate us. Being able to go fast occasionally also helps for the very long runs and outrunning bad weather. We just see too many folks on boats that are too big, even though they would probably never admit it.

We like anchoring out a lot. However, for us, sightseeing and meeting new folks is our main focus. The sightseeing portion is focused on places that we wouldn't normally go via car. We did make a point of visiting Ground Zero, New York City, due to the emotional nature of that tragic event.

Life is a continuous journey into the unknown; the idea of this trip wasn't even in our gray matter earlier in our lives. Risk analysis should, of course, be done for any proposed venture, so that adds to why we chose the Loop for a year-long trip versus taking a Jet Ski across the ocean for our first trip.

We are strong in our faiths; so one objective of our trip was to have many discussions, with each other and those we met, on the world, and what makes humans tick with respect to their individual preferences. So far, we have concluded that people are more spiritual than they are willing to admit. It is such a personal thing that discussing it with strangers seems to be an embarrassment to them, so they avoid the subject – a sign of our times – being afraid to offend?

We know that this is a very personal thing, so we try our best not to put our influence or choice of religion into this comment. However, having faith and spirituality just isn't enough without practicing it everyday in some form. For us, this may include attending services as often as we can during the trip, daily readings, or prayer time. However, I digress.

We have had family and friends join us, but the effort to coordinate with landlubbers (John calls them earth-people) seems too difficult. They are used to pinpoint timing and locations, by way of travel agents, but pinpoint timing just cannot be done on this trip. However, each visitor we've had has been great, and we loved having them and hope for more. Once they get to the boat and see the logistics are straightforward, they seem to settle in just fine. However, we are pleasers, so the stress can be great, as we want our guests to enjoy the trip, and we have a tendency to want to entertain them. In sum, my thoughts on this are to not push people to visit you on the boat. Make it very clear to the ones you want to invite that you'd love them to visit, but clearly place the ball in their court to call you for arrangements/planning. Do your best to explain to them what to expect – be very clear and blunt if you think they are being unrealistic about the lifestyle.

How goes traveling with a mate? We play a lot of games together, which is much better than just watching the TV. We have found, when we travel, we enjoy each other's company more than the TV, so even when we have cable at marinas, we don't even hook it up unless there is something VERY special on like an Auburn football game. We play lots of competitive games, such as Scrabble and Suduko puzzles, to keep the juices flowing between us. One thing for certain is that while experiencing a trip like this, a marriage is sure to get stronger. If a couple has a weak marriage, they probably aren't even going to attempt a trip of this nature because they will see the potential for disaster. However, we do see a stray couple or two that makes us wonder why they are doing the Loop. For the most though, we were pleased to see that the majority of the relationships were positive and supportive.

As with most boaters, the man was the main dreamer in this family. However, Sue, being a big time adventurer, was ready to do it too, as she has previously done things like white water rafting overnight, drove NASCAR etc. So a new adventure was up her alley even though it meant being away from the grandkids. John had dreamed of long-term boating ever since he was in high school, while owning a boat three years before he bought his first car. His dreams were typical of a youngster imagining far off places, dreaming of meeting pirates, girls, and experiencing what the locals at far-off, distant places do. Except for the girls (he has the best and does not look anymore) the dreams are still as strong as ever.

John's thought processes (his mind is always racing) is that dreams beget goals that beget plans that beget implementation. Most dreams don't come true, but are good exercises. However, we also think that if you focus and follow up with some action, who knows what can happen. For example, making sure you plan for retirement so you can experience new things. Planning on retirement didn't mean that the boat trip would occur, but if we never retired, many of our dreams would never be possible, and setting a goal such as a trip like this just becomes a frustrating experience. Plans are just that. Beginning to learn about the goal, reading, talking to folks, taking classes, learning new skills, prototyping the idea to see if your dream/goal was real and, in the end, even desirable. For example, John at one time thought he'd like to learn to fly. After going up with some folks and interviewing others, he decided nope, that dream can just stay a dream. So, the plan, which had become a goal, now is just a dream again. Make sense? This particular type of trip we dreamed of was all about discovering that one could make a continuous Loop and not have to backtrack. Thus, all travel would be a new experience versus simply traveling back over waters that were just navigated in order to get back home.

John, through observations and his experience as a Hospice volunteer, thinks that 75 is the age at which most folks lose the ability to do the things (achieve the goals) they want to, either physically or financially. Retiring at 52 was risky, but so far it's good for us. He figured that from52 to 55, he would concentrate on how to be a retiree (which is another story). Then from 55 to 75 (20 years) meant that four percent of his remaining useful life was going to be burned up each year. If he died before 75, that would be God's will and he would be happy with his decisions, because he was doing his best to enjoy life. If he lived beyond75, which is what usually happens, AND was healthy, then that would be truly a gift from God for him to enjoy these bonus years with his loved ones. No money at that time? Well, we all have to take risks, and this is a calculated one as we aren't rich folks. Just like taking the Loop is a risk, so is security in retirement.

Nothing MADE us do this other than our lives brought us here, and upon arrival, it felt good. No one was going to get hurt by us making this trip, in fact, this is the first time that our daughter has been on her own with her family, so new growth has been experienced by all of us with respect to being apart. We always know that we are within a day or two of getting to each other if need be, and part of loving someone is supporting his or her dreams and goals. Our kids have a goal of owning their own home, so living in our home while we were gone, is helping them achieve that goal by learning and saving money. It has been great watching our kids mature with us being gone - they are learning new things on their own, and we also learn we don't have to be there for them to get along. However, missing some of the things that are happening in their lives can be a little tough at times.

We had many conversations with friends and family, and came to realize how the potential for enriching several lives, in addition to our own, was possible. We feel that when we finish our trip, we will be more effective in our relationships and in our next adventure, which may mean adjusting our volunteering efforts to fit our goals better versus things that we feel we were roped into. On a tough note, we also have learned that maybe someone who we considered a friend was not. This may be a conclusion we came to, or they did. It has been interesting to see how they have responded. We have been surprised on both sides - that is folks who we considered acquaintances have become close, and vice versa.

John & Sue Winter - *Miss Liberty*

Typical comments of family and friends: "Why would you want to do this?" Life is short - more importantly, why would one not want to take on a new adventure? "Won't you be bored?" Yes, but surely not as much as if we stayed home and did the same thing every day? John's definition of insanity is doing the same things repeatedly, and getting the same results each time. "How can you stand each other for that length of time?" If a marriage isn't strong enough to take on new adventures, then the marriage is probably doomed to be a bad one anyway. "How can you afford to do this?" We can't financially but we cannot afford to lay around waiting to die either. Lastly, "We are jealous - in a good way - what can we do to help your dream come true?" Many have been there for our kids, keeping our cars at their place, prayer lists at church, keeping mail, living in our home, calling, and e-mail... What a great feeling.

What are the disadvantages? Mostly expected things, like the cramped quarters, having to always move things out of the way in order to get to the things we needed to get to, not having that favorite pot to cook in, and missing the table saw in the basement back home. However, not having these things to be tied to is sometimes a good thing. For example, as much as John likes golf and his newspaper, he isn't missing them because this Loop experience is too fantastic. In fact, we are convinced that when we get back home, there will be things that we had liked that we won't want to do any more, as we learn more of what we have come to enjoy. As mentioned above, we feel that each day, we grow closer to each other. We have more in-depth discussions about what is important in our lives, and continue to wonder why so many people in the world aren't happy. Life is easy; it's just that many make it difficult for themselves.

We refuse to let our worst experience affect us in a negative way. We choose to have those as growth experiences instead. Outside of experiencing some bad weather conditions, having to call the Coast Guard on Lake Michigan, calling the Coast Guard to check on us three times on the Delaware River, taking on water on the Hudson River, having to make emergency repairs to keep the boat afloat, losing a transmission on Lake Michigan, and repairs that continually are needed, we feel that we have no major worst experiences. We hear of folks saying that this marina or that marina is bad due to attitudes, facilities, or prices, but the way we figure it, this is part of the experience. If you take the time to see what makes a person tick on any particularly day, and enjoy them for what they have to offer, then even the worst of marina attendants or owners can be enjoyable.

We all have bad days. For example, we came across one marina manager who had lost a loved one to an untimely death at an early age. Once we knew that, then understanding them was easy, and by the time we left that marina, we were best of friends. Of course, missing family, having to put our beloved pet down (18 years old) was no fun. In addition, doing the Mississippi and Ohio Rivers during a flood stage was also not fun.

Best experience includes all the fantastic people we have met, and many of them that will be friends, hopefully, for life. Also, we enjoyed experiencing all the new history and cultures we encountered. We are continually amazed at the fun of navigating, and enjoy the challenges of finding our way around, watching out for things from crab pots to shoals, and plotting new courses, which are all different from one body of water to the next.

One thing that we learned not to worry about was the cost. We aren't rich folks by any means. However, we learned that, except for the gas prices going up during the trip, budgeting was easy because we looked at only the incremental costs of the trip versus living at home and taking our regular vacations, and fixing up the home that most folks normally do. So, when looking at gas prices (remember, we are gas, not diesel) we concluded that even for an extra $5,000, that was an insignificant incremental cost.

After reading all those folks' comments in the AGLCA newsletter that have completed the Loop, stating their favorite places, we have concluded that listing favorites takes away from the overall trip. So, there is no favorite place or places for us. However, we are amazed of the places that we have found to be gems that folks don't rave about as much, talk about, or even go to.

The rivers of North Carolina are amazing, including the Outer Banks. We traveled the Pamlico and Albemarle Rivers, for example, all the way to their ends – really worth it. The Long Island Sound offered so much. The Champlain Route versus the Erie is a must-do route. We visited so many little bergs; many residents came down to our boat and welcomed us to their town.

However, so far, the Illinois River has been the biggest surprise. We spent two weeks visiting the small towns and anchorages, even though the river is only three 300 miles long. We met mayors, police chiefs, and Commerce Department folks, all who welcomed us with open arms. There is much history here too.

We have decided that bypassing the Big Bend of Florida will be a mistake, and thus are committed to visiting them, even though almost all Loopers pass over that area. We are so disappointed that we didn't do any of the New Jersey ICW based on Looper input.

So, what is the favorite? None. Lesson learned: Do not bypass ANYPLACE just because someone told you to, such as many of the rivers off the Tennessee, including going to Knoxville and its side rivers, or the State of Georgia side channels.

What do we hope to gain from this? We want to achieve the goal we set for ourselves; we want to feel that satisfaction of accomplishment. We really wanted to, and did, meet many nice folks from many different places. Of course, we valued the learning of new cultures, histories, and seeing what nature has to offer. We also hope that when this adventure is over and we meet our maker, that we have nothing but good feelings about how we lived our lives, including the selfish things we did for ourselves. We know that if we only did things for our own satisfaction, that our lives wouldn't be whole. However, by doing things also for ourselves, by taking care of ourselves, then we will be able to take care of others, or serve others, hopefully in a better way. Some people would call this "the complete package." Since we are about 60% complete, we are gaining everyday, including in our marriage. It is amazing to us sometimes how our love for each other grows. We WANT to go out of our ways to help each other.

Cairo Bridge - Ohio River, Illinois

Ann, Joey, Will & John Spinetto - *Family Matters*
Banner Elk, North Carolina

John and I are NOT boaters. We have never owned a boat larger than our canoe. When we decided to do the Loop, family and friends thought we were nuts. Of course, the idea of embarking on a boat journey the magnitude of the Loop was one thing – but doing it on a 65-foot boat with two kids on board seemed to be insane.

We began the process much like others. We read *Honey, Let's Get a Boat,* by Ron and Eva Stob. The Loop loomed "out there" as something we would do "someday." Then, we lost our 30-year-old daughter to brain cancer. It was a wake-up call. Life is full of unexpected things and a carpe diem attitude took hold. We weren't getting any younger and the boys were growing older so quickly. A year of working, playing, and experiencing each day as a family just seemed too good to be true.

We started in the summer by taking a powerboat course through the Annapolis Powerboat School. We learned the basics of how to maneuver a twin-engine powerboat, as well as some of the rudimentary rules of the sea. While cruising the Chesapeake Bay, we observed different makes of boats, and determined that a Hatteras was our best bet for the Loop. (This was based on the boxy lines of older Hatteras yachts resembling the lines of my Chevy Suburban at home!)

I called the Hatteras headquarters when we returned and asked to speak to the marketing director. I asked her point blank, "We are interested in buying a Hatteras, how do I find one?" She put me in touch with a wonderful broker in Baltimore and our search for a boat began. Chuck Meyers, our broker, had the patience of Job. We were complete neophytes in the boating world, and he educated us. We went to numerous boat shows together (Annapolis, Miami, and Fort Lauderdale). In January, we found our dreamboat, a 60-foot Hatteras Extended Deck. They say one of the happiest days in your life is the day you buy a boat, and it was.

Our boat was actually 65-foot from bowsprit to swim platform, a very large boat for a first-time boat owner. We made several modifications before we could even begin to practice aboard her. It was 23 feet to the top of the radar domes on the arch. In order to fit the boat under the 19-foot fixed bridge in Chicago, we had to have the arch cut and hinged. We also added bow thrusters for better maneuverability. She also needed a minor rebuild on her port engine. We added a new windlass and a whopping 30 feet of anchor chain, with a new Danforth anchor. Lastly, we changed the name of our beautiful vessel to *Family Matters*. The boat was finally ready for our training in April.

John spent several weekends with our training captain. The boys and I joined the fun when soccer games didn't get in the way. Finally, May 23rd, we shoved off from our dock in Morehead City, North Carolina, and headed north.

Words cannot even begin to describe the adventure that we had over the next year. Our time with each other and the kids was more precious than all the gold in the world. We would not trade a single day – the memories are incredible.

As a Mom, one thing on our trip that I treasured was the quality of family time. Our experience seemed to be quite different from other Loopers in that at the end of a day of cruising, other Loopers would relax with a drink and that wonderful Looper camaraderie. We, on the other hand, wouldn't be relaxing with a drink. Oh no, the second half of our day was just beginning.

Upon docking or anchoring, the bikes came off, the dinghy came down, or the kayaks were lowered. There was no rest for the weary. Yet this was the most rewarding part of our journey. I remember many a time waving to the rest of the Loopers happily sipping their cocktails, while we zipped the boys around on their inner tube and wake board.

There were other times where we took a carpe diem approach to school. Upon arriving in a new town, we would visit the local museum or historic site or natural wonder. Having an AAA tour book along helped enormously in finding our way around unfamiliar territory. For example, while on the Erie Canal, I read about the Herkimer Diamond Mines. We arrived at the Herkimer dock early in the day, too early to dock for the night. We tied up at the dock and entered the gift shop. There, we inquired about how to get a cab to the mines. The woman working the shop offered us the keys to her car, saying she didn't get off until 4 p.m.. She gave us directions to the mine and to the local Wal-Mart (always a necessary stop when in a car) and away we went. We spent several hours visiting the mine and doing necessary shopping. We returned the car, hopped back on the boat, and continued on our way. Having the boys along gave us the incentive to really explore towns in ways that we may not have otherwise done.

For the first four months on our trip, our satellite TV wasn't working; a blessing for which I am truly thankful! After dinner, our family would enjoy a game of cards or Scrabble. At bedtime, I would sit in the hall between the boys' rooms and read to them. Some nights, we would just sit up top and enjoy the stars and the beauty of our surroundings.

One evening, while anchored in the islands of the North Channel (the most northern point of our trip), we decided to have a dance lesson with the boys. We would be arriving in Mackinaw Island in a week or so, and spending a week at the Grand Hotel. The boys needed to be ready. It is one of my most cherished memories - dancing on the upper deck of *Family Matters* under the stars, with the boat gently swinging at anchor, in the evening breeze, with my three favorite men.

The following May, we pulled back into the very same dock we had left one year earlier in Morehead City, North Carolina. We wonder why anyone would have a boat only to come back to the same place every night. What a waste of a wonderful way to travel. Each day was an adventure. Each day, we woke up wondering what interesting people, places, and sights would be around the bend. What would our dock or anchorage look like tonight? Today might just be the best one yet... and it always was!

We unpacked the boat the next day and drove home. We never saw *Family Matters* again. Remember, we are not boaters. We are family, and this is why we did the Loop. You can always have an excuse not to go... All we can say is DO IT! Get out of your box and DO IT! The Loop is waiting.

Tennessee River Anchorage

Todd O. Smith - *E*GRESS
Wabasha, Minnesota

Having grown up on the waters of the upper Mississippi, I've had dreams of heading down the river on a great adventure. I had suppressed those ambitions long ago, because of the circumstances that most of us find ourselves in early on in adulthood. I was busy. My wife, Kate, and I took up sailing on a lake that the Mississippi River goes through, and the commercial traffic that we saw was a constant reminder that this river actually leads to faraway places. Now that our kids are grown and long gone, I grew tired of sailing within the confines of this lake, and I was up for the adventure I had dreamed of long ago. My wife and I talked about taking a trip like this when we bought our present boat, but the closer it came to actually doing it, she seemed less exited about it and finally, she said she couldn't do it but if I wanted to go alone, it was alright with her. I didn't need to be told twice.

I left on my adventure from Pepin, Wisconsin, on the upper Mississippi River, heading downriver. I arrived at the Gulf of Mexico by the normal Tennessee-Tombigbee Waterway route, and then I went down to the Florida Keys, up to New York, the Hudson River, Erie Canal, Oswego Canal, and Trent-Severn Waterway. I took the small craft route through Georgian Bay when depth allowed, and looped out into the bay when it didn't. My route was not the normal

Loop as there was one portage, from Duluth, Minnesota to Hudson, Wisconsin. That portion had to be done by truck.

My intent was to take the North Channel to Lake Michigan, to Chicago, and the Illinois River and the Mississippi River back home, but at that time I was starting to get requests from my other half to be home a bit earlier. Instead I sailed up to Sault Ste. Marie to Lake Superior, and west to Duluth. After a 100-mile portage to Hudson, Wisconsin, the boat was put back in the water on the St. Croix River, and it was a short 60 miles down to my homeport of Pepin, Wisconsin.

My vessel is a 24-year-old, 30-foot sailboat with plenty of room for one additional crew member. More than that would have made it a bit tight with all the extra gear I needed for the trip. It has an adequate galley, head, and sleeping accommodations. The only electrical supply, when not in port, came from one house battery and one starting battery. These were charged with the engine generator or shore power. I had a small propane camp heater that proved to be less than capable of keeping the cabin warm on really chilly evenings, and I also had the alcohol galley stove that threw out a lot more heat.

The coldest evenings were designated as baking nights. Of course, neither of these could be used at night while sleeping, so some mornings were a bit brisk. When I was on shore power, I had a small electric heater that kept the cabin toasty, and seemed like a real luxury. I was without refrigeration for the first eight months until I purchased a power cooler that served me well. I just got tired of trying to find ice every couple of days. Overall, I'd say most people would describe my accommodations as "Spartan."

I took this trip alone, although I had visitors at various ports along the way. I also had friends and relatives that jumped on as crew on occasion. Out of the 11 months of the entire trip, I had visitors or crew members for about 60 days.

Having others to share the trip with me was the best time of those 11 months. During the times I was in port for a day or so, without any crew on board, I was treated to the social contact that I craved. Just a chance to have a discussion that got a verbal response was great. This was also the case when I was traveling with other boats, as it made for someone to enjoy a beer with, and a little conversation at the end of the day. There were many days of traveling alone that were tremendously lonely, especially those days that I was anchored out in a remote area, and would get up the next day to get some more miles behind me.

When I had someone else on board, the constant companionship made the traveling and other shore side adventures that much better.

I must admit though, after spending a week or more with someone I wasn't used to living that closely with, I was sometimes longing for those days when I didn't have to contend with anyone else's habits, gear, or idiosyncrasies in my small living space. What's that they say about visitors and fish?

I thought life on board was enjoyable. My living space was small but the actual day-to-day exercises that you have to go through didn't present any major problems because of those physical limitations. I had an electric water heater that was good in port, but otherwise I had to heat my water on the stove for all my washing needs. Doing those tasks took a little longer, but I had plenty of time to do them. I could do a lot of that while I was traveling once I got my auto helm (Otto) on board. (I wouldn't recommend that anyone take this trip solo without this little device). With this gear installed, I found that I could easily get something prepared or cleaned up in the galley as long as I still kept a vigilant eye on my course.

The most common comment from family and friends was, "Wow! That sounds like a great trip. A once in a lifetime adventure." What usually followed when they found out I was going alone and the time it was going to take was, "What does Kate think about this?" Another comment I got often was, "Are you looking for crew? God, I'd love to go on part of it." I later found out that this response was just "bar talk." When I would follow up on it later, there always seemed to be a good reason why they couldn't make it. I don't remember many negative comments. The strangest one I heard was from another sailor from my home harbor. He said, "Why don't you just ship the boat down and meet it there. It'll save you that long trip down the river." What was he thinking?

I'm not sure that I had that much in the way of expectations. I was looking for a great adventure, and I was confident that I wouldn't be disappointed. I expected that there would be many things that would go wrong, and that it would tax my problem-solving capabilities. But that's what adventure is all about. Put yourself out there to be tested, and be confident that you'll get through and live to see the next test. I thought that I would meet many friendly and kind people; in this my expectations were far exceeded.

Other projects that, in the normal living environment, get barely a thought become major deals because they involve traveling away from the boat and transporting a bit of freight. Grocery shopping and laundry are tops on this list. In some places that I traveled, getting fuel was a problem. On the upper Mississippi, it's difficult to find diesel at the marinas. There were many places where I had to strap a fuel tank on my bicycle and find a station that sold it. As anyone can imagine, five gallons of diesel tends to throw off the bicycle balance pretty easily. The hills are major obstacles in both directions. All of these inconveniences and tasks were accepted as the normal exercises of my new life on the water.

I'm hard pressed to come up with my worst and best experiences. The main candidate for the worst? I'd say it was when I was struck by another boat during some bad wind in an anchorage in Atlantic Highlands, New Jersey. The mooring shackle had broken on the offending boat, and there was no one on board as it was being blown through the anchorage. I came on deck, after hearing a very loud crash, to find a boat that weighed three times the weight of mine, tangled in my bow pulpit. I managed to get it freed without breaking my leg, and as I was pushing it off, I felt a tinge of guilt about letting it blow toward the leeward rocky shore, but I didn't think I had a lot of options. It went aground shortly after that and had to be pulled off during the windstorm in the middle of the night.

The section of the trip I liked the best was the Trent-Severn Waterway. I loved the spectacular beauty of all those rivers and lakes. The old, manually operated locks were so nice and laid back, and the cities and towns were easy to access. The two hydraulic lift locks were quite interesting, and the marine railway "the Big Chute" was a real hoot.

The best part of the trip was when I talked my wife into coming along from Savannah to Charleston. We had a great time exploring the cities in that stretch together.

I think what I gained during this adventure was a confidence in myself, and in what my boat could handle. I know there's nothing our home sailing area can throw at me that will be anywhere near what I saw out on my trip. I should have expected it, but I was somewhat surprised that I very rarely went out sailing for fun as I do when sailing at home. Sailing became a mode of transportation, and doing it for fun had very little appeal.

I found out that I really like to sail on an inland lake where I don't have any specific distance that I have to make that day, and all I have to do is a little sail handling while sitting back and enjoying the day. That's one of the unexpected benefits I've discovered since being back, but I don't think that is something that would stop me from going again. I'll just know what to expect next time.

Bridge on the Tennessee-Tombigbee Waterway

Cindy & Frank Staffe - $\mathcal{P}$EACEKEEPER
Green Cove Spring, Florida

Frank –

Our plan was to live and travel by boat for at least 10 years. Deciding to start by doing the Loop was an opportunity to get a lot of experience behind us since we plan to spend a lot of time in the Abacos and Exhumes afterwards, to fulfill our plan of living aboard after completing an adventure of a lifetime. We plan to go to Maine, for lobsters, to see more of the Chesapeake Bay, and the Gulf of Mexico.

Our boat is a 44-foot Endeavor, Trawler Cat with a 19-foot beam and three-foot draft. As for accommodations, use your imagination; we are able to have more on the boat than we had in our home. It is very spacious.

The decision to leave the comforts of a land-based home was not hard. All material things in life can be replaced. "Life only happens once, doesn't last very long and the only sure thing about it is that you won't get out of it alive. So, make the best of it" This was always a dream of mine, to live and travel on a boat. It took some time to get our family to understand my quote above. Once they did, they were all for it. Besides, look at all the different places that they can visit us for a free vacation.

Well, that thought sold them. Many of our friends stated that they wished they had the nerve to take the trip themselves. I suppose I was lucky. I grew up never being afraid of the unknown, and was always willing to take on a new challenge.

We did not set out to gain anything special from this adventure. It was just a new way of living, no hassles on freeways and not having to rush anywhere. If an anchorage looked nice, we would stay for a while – then move on. I need to add though; this life is not all peaches and cream.

Bad weather on a boat is not a pleasant experience. Many things break down, or need to be replaced. It costs a lot and it is often hard to crawl into the small spaces to fix or replace parts. We boaters learn to adapt and be very patient. I do find life on the water to move slower, and it seems the people one meets on the water are far more friendlier, willing to help and are more understanding than those non-boaters we meet on land. Why is this? I think because we all have grown up and learned to enjoy every day for itself. Oh, and best of all, most of us are retired. That helps.

Living on the boat with my wife and dog is no problem. That is why we choose a catamaran. There is plenty of room for all three of us to have our space when we need it. It has been 17 months now and it has been the very best.

The best experience we gained definitely was meeting people from all over the world. The only worst experience was being in a storm with 15 to 20-foot waves breaking over the helm, in the Atlantic Ocean, off South Carolina, and only having had about a month's worth of experience on the boat before that happened.

As of this writing, we have not experienced our favorite area, and we think that is, in part, because we have not reached the Bahamas yet. Walking on white sand beaches, lying in the sun all day, eating fresh lobster and fish. What more could one have? Oh, by the way, no one should have to live like this, but some of us have to do it for the others that can't.

Cindy –

When Frank and I decided to live on *Peacekeeper*, our boat, I told him this is for at least a five-year duration. We wanted to give ourselves a chance to experience the live aboard, boating lifestyle. First, we would do the Great Loop, then whatever sounds good after that.

We left our family back home, wondering whether or not they would ever see us again. They were sad, excited, and jealous, but they gave us their blessings. We have made two trips back to visit and I'm sure there are more to come. Now they realize that we are not far away. The tears they shed of sadness when we left turn to tears of joy when we arrive.

The experience of boating in all kinds of waters is remarkable. All of the classes we took through the Power Squadron helped a great deal, and everything you learn eventually comes to life out on the water. I never imagined us piloting a boat this big until the day we launched the boat. Some days are calm and peaceful, others, a new challenge, but every day is a great experience.

Frank and I have learned to enjoy each other more in smaller environs. We joke, laugh at each other, listen to one another complain, then look at each other and laugh. I often said to Frank, "Don't talk to me for one-half-an-hour." This seems to work well. How many times can you ask where someone is going when you live in an 836-square-foot space, and are anchored out. Unless you see me getting into the dinghy or jumping into the water, I am not going far.

My number one pet peeve is... spiders. You notice spiders more in certain parts of the country than you do living in a house.

Our dog, Diamond, adjusted well on the trip. She lays on the front bow under the seats for shade when it is sunny. We still have to dinghy her to land when at anchor. This becomes more of a job for Frank because when it is early morning and it is cool, you just want to stay in bed, then late in the evenings, when it is dark, you don't want to have to go out and take a walk or dinghy to shore.

Best times, as Frank mentioned, were all the friendly people we met. As far as places we saw and enjoyed, they are: stops on the Chesapeake Bay such as St Michaels (reminded us of the Caribbean), Chesapeake City, Maryland; the Erie Canal, and all the quaint little towns there are along the way.

We traveled from Waterford all the way to Buffalo, New York on the canal, with so many small towns to stop and enjoy. So peaceful. Not everyone decided to go the east route of the Erie Canal, we are glad we didn't miss it.

The worst experience for us was when we were out in the Atlantic Ocean and encountered a storm. We were scared. It was not a pleasant trip. With only one hour away from port, it seemed more like 24 hours. Diamond didn't know what to think or do. The waves were so big; hitting us so hard that our refrigerator broke loose from the frame and a rack broke loose and fell.

Also, while on the Tennessee-Tombigbee Waterway, we wanted to anchor at Chickasaw Bayou for the night, but the water depth, which was charted to be five feet, was only two feet, so we moved and dropped anchor at the mouth, outside the channel, next to Red Nun around 6 a.m. All this while having to hail the tows to let them know we were there. Frank stayed up all night to watch and warn the tow traffic.

The next stop for us will be to spend five months in the Bahamas. After that, wherever Cindy would like to go we will go. We will ad lib every day until we get tired, or health problems prevent us from going any further.

Tennessee-Tombigbee Waterway

Mike & Carol Gordon - *E*VELYN J
Fairhope, Alabama

We departed from our homeport of Fairhope, Alabama, in March, heading counter-clockwise on the Great Loop, returning in November of that same year. We were aboard a 47-foot Nordhavn trawler with two staterooms and two heads. It was very comfortable with all of the creature comforts, but the downside was a deep draft (six feet) and healthy mast height (up 31 feet/ down 19 feet.).

We both had intense careers, but together we possessed a vision to get out early enough to enjoy the fruits of our labor. We embarked on this trip for the pure adventure of it, the fun of exploring the unknown, the challenge of learning and seeing new things, and we were most intrigued by the idea of exploring this country by its earliest easy mode of transportation… the waterways.

One of us (to this day it is still under debate who) read an article about the Great Loop and America's Great Loop Cruisers' Association (AGLCA). We ordered and read the book *Honey, Let's Get a Boat*, by Ron and Eva Stob, joined the association, and attended several Trawler Fests and boat shows. We soaked up information while we secretly planned our big escape from the daily work world.

We retired within days of one another (ages 47 and 57) and immersed ourselves in the search for "THE BOAT." That took a year, along with selling the "THE BIG HOUSE." Then we ordered our boat and signed up for Chapman's School of Seamanship, and took a three-month Professional Mariners course to better prepare. Along with this course, we both obtained our captain's license. After a lengthy commissioning process, and a two-week, pre-cruise, christening party, we moved to our new coastal home, and while still sorting out the details, we got underway.

Our family and close friends generally had one of two reactions: They either wished they could do likewise or they thought we were nuts! The most common comment from the latter group was that the trip was too long, with probably too much togetherness.

We were alone, without guests for the majority of the time, but had at least three friends who each joined us for three-week stints.

We gained a whole new set of friends on our trip, met lots of very interesting people, saw some unique small places (Oriental, North Carolina, and Charlevoix, Michigan) and had time to explore some larger cities that we would have missed (Toronto, Ontario, and Cleveland, Ohio). However, we expected all that to come from this adventure.

What was unexpected was the amount of knowledge, and confidence of our skill sets that we gained. We learned how to handle, maintain, and troubleshoot problems aboard as they arose. We know way more about the generation and management of electricity than we ever dreamed of, computer issues don't intimidate us anymore, maintaining a complicated "system" like a water maker, air conditioning, inverter, or even entertainment system seems much less daunting than it appeared several years ago. We can plot a course, set electronic waypoints, back it up with the paper charts, and identify vessels on the waterway at night by their lights.

Additionally, we further strengthened our marriage and relationship. Each relied on the other to help shoulder the load of planning and maintaining our adventure. We did a good job of sharing the responsibilities, and it took both of us to do it.

Our consistent description of life aboard was "comfortable" and that was by design. We were surprised to learn that Mike is more of a homebody, and I am more of a nomad. At the conclusion of the trip, Mike declared that we weren't taking any trips longer than 10 days away from home, while I was ready to go around the Loop again, tomorrow. HOWEVER, if we hadn't done it, we wouldn't have known.

We got along remarkably well, but did struggle with letting the boat "run us" instead of running it. We confess to having moments of being overwhelmed by the planning, boat maintenance, transportation logistics, and general upkeep that this trip required. Upon reflection, I think this reaction was normal.

Our best experience is tough to narrow down, but definitely would be one of these: trading beers for local crab in May Port, Florida, cracking them open on the stern, and having the best fresh crab omelet for dinner; or biking around Clear Lake, Michigan, and happening upon a sailboat regatta, getting invited aboard to crew, and flying the spinnaker while taking first place. Or perhaps hooking up with new friends in Dover, Canada, to attend "Todd's Bar and Grille", a sweet set up in Todd's backyard garden shack, while his spouse had "Sally's Liquid Cinema" on Wednesday nights, DVDs projected on the shack. We missed a showing of JAWS the week before, shown while the audience sat in lawn chairs in Lake Ontario.

Looking back, our best experiences were the impromptu happenings that you stumble upon if you are open to the possibilities.

Our worst experience was Charleston, South Carolina, not the city, which we love, but the boating experience. It started with our early morning off shore arrival in 10-foot seas, listening to a sinking sailboat talk to the USCG. Our vessel took the seas well (the wave period was very short), but the dark, the tossing, and the desperate radio conversation made it intense. After a wonderful two weeks in Charleston, South Carolina, including the great Spoleto Festival, we departed on a bad note also. Extremely swift currents in the harbor swept us into an expensive sport fisherman that didn't enjoy the contact. I (Carol) was driving and was crushed that I had actually crushed another boat!

Two areas were our favorites for the same reason: North Carolina and the entire eastern shore of Lake Michigan. We enjoyed the quaint communities that took pride in their beautification, supported local arts, and fostered a sense of community. Both of these locations harbored many examples of these traits. Frankly, they reminded us of our own chosen community in Fairhope, where we closed our adventure in November, nine months after leaving.

Tarpon Springs, Florida

Dick & Diane Hanson -ᔑOUVENIR
Woodbury, Minnesota

Dick –

Our Great Loop trip was a planned family experience, but the seven additional trips between Minnesota and Florida have not only involved, but also depended upon, our network of boating friends that has grown as a result of our Great Loop stories. So, our primary thought on who we made the trip with is that a completely unimagined value has greatly expanded our social perspective of shared experiences.

Souvenir was purchased new, specifically for our Great Loop adventure. It's a 2001 Carver Model 506 aft-cabin motor yacht. In hindsight, we believe it was "meant to be," and we've been very blessed that it was.

My retirement dream was built around this boat, which met our requirements of being very comfortable, all-weather, self-sufficient, maintainable, capable of 20 miles per hour cruise speed, and ample storage. But not bigger than 50 feet long, 20-one feet high, or four-and-a-half-foot draft (that's exactly what it is), within a defined financial plan/budget that included a trade-in houseboat, both stable and maneuverable. We've put 1700 engine hours and 20,000 miles on it in four years, and it's been perfect for us, for the way we've used it.

Technically, our Loop, as planned and nearly as completed, was measured from the mouth of the Illinois River at Mile 218 on the Upper

Mississippi, down to Key West, Florida in February. Then we traveled up the East Coast to New York City on the Fourth of July, up the Hudson River to the Erie/Oswego Canals, back across the Great Lakes via the "southern route" (Welland Canal to Lake Erie, and around Michigan to Green Bay, Wisconsin). Then we continued to Chicago and the Cal-Sag Sanitary Canal, and the Illinois River back to its mouth, for 5,736 statute miles in 10 months, 20-three days, and one hour.

The one piece of the plan we didn't complete was a 10-day excursion to the Bahamas. We sat in Fort Lauderdale, Florida, in March, waiting for a weather window to cross the Gulf Stream without success, and we finally decided to just start heading north. The primary reason we took the "southern route" across the Great Lakes was to visit friends in Buffalo, New York; Cleveland, Ohio; and Detroit, Michigan. This decision was made easier as we read reports from Loopers of low water on the "northern route" (Trent-Severn Waterway/Georgian Bay, Canada) and lots of prop work required on boats with more than a four-foot draft.

After 30 years of family vacations house boating on local rivers (within a 100 miles of St. Paul, Minnesota), we were dedicated marina/river-rats. One of our good boating friends had made the trip between Minnesota and Florida several times, including something referred to as The Great Loop. In the mid-nineties, approximately five years before I expected to retire, I became aware of, and read Ron and Eva Stob's book, *Honey, Let's Get a Boat*, and I was hooked. I became Member #502 of the America's Great Loop Cruisers' Association (AGLCA) to get the newsletters, and began serious research and planning for my retirement dream. "Embarking on the unknown," became a passion, leaving the "certainty" of my home was never an issue, and family and friends have been an integral part of the trip.

I have since learned to appreciate my wife's interest and willingness to go along with my passion, not realizing before how rare that is, even among supposedly dedicated boating families. Most guys who would like to never get to do this! Much of our success on our trip I attribute to her requirement for a clear understanding of some basic "rules of engagement" up front, e.g. at least every two months we would leave the boat for service, and take a one-way rental car home to visit family for two to four weeks. We did that at Destin, and Fort Lauderdale, Florida, Norfolk, Virginia, and in the Detroit, Michigan area. Another critical rule was: We would never depart a safe harbor if forecast seas were more than three feet, and if actual seas were more than five feet, we would abort and find a safe harbor. The latter happened only twice.

My son and daughter, now in their mid-thirties, had grown up around rivers, marinas, and boats. They both worked weekends and summers at our marina for six to eight years during their teens and early twenties. My daughter's twins (a boy and a girl) are on the same path, now 14, and they were the perfect age and mind-set to join us. So, in June, we left *Souvenir* in the Norfolk area for our "home visit." When we returned, they came with us, and after a couple of days seeing the sights in Washington, DC, they came on board for seven weeks till our next "home visit" from Detroit. My single son, who lives and works in Manhattan, visited us in Baltimore, Maryland, and then hosted us for a spectacular week in New York City over the Fourth of July. We both have mothers in their nineties. Mine was an experienced traveler, originally from Minnesota and Iowa, who lived in Florida, near water, during her retirement years. Diane's is from Delaware, with the ocean/beach always a big part of her life. So, they were both very interested in our adventure, and thrilled for our opportunity.

A big percentage of our friends are boaters, of course, and those who aren't are very familiar with our boating history, in many cases, having shared experiences. Of course, our list of friends has grown dramatically during and since our Great Loop adventure. They all, especially through the magic of e-mail and our website, have been virtually involved. And I've kept a list of the guys who have said, "Wow! I'll never be able to do that, but let me know if you ever need help with a leg."

During my fall and spring migrations between Minnesota and Florida since completion of our Great Loop, I've had 12 different first mates, while Diane drives the car, with the family pet. It's a win/win situation, and everybody LOVES it, especially the stay-at-home wives of my first mates! I have an on-going list of candidates, and have to be careful how I "select" my crew, so as not to offend those who don't get to go.

I wish I could articulate, "What I have gained from this experience." My words both written and verbal seem so inadequate. First, as a life-long boater in love with the water and all the good things in life that go with it, I have a huge feeling of accomplishment with a true once-in-a-lifetime experience. Secondly, the relationships it has already, and continues to spawn; not only enhancing those that we had, but also building on the new ones. It's a whole new dimension of our social life, and three years later, it continues to amaze me how often I'm approached by a stranger who is aware of our trip by word-of-mouth, or from our website. People even see our boat name, *Souvenir*, and say, "I've heard of you and your travels." We got a Christmas card one year from a couple we couldn't remember meeting. Of course, it often comes up in conversations with new people we've met in entirely different circumstances.

Another major benefit has been a completely new perspective on the geography, history, and the diverse cultures of our great country. I have traveled extensively by conventional modes throughout my life. However, to experience it from the water in our own boat is a new dimension. Just a small, but very concrete example is passing under magnificent highway bridges that we've driven over many times. Some of my favorite pictures are of the underside of the Chesapeake Bay Bridge, the new C&D Canal and old St. George's bridges in Delaware, the bridges of New York City, "Big Mack" (the Mackinaw bridge), etc, etc. In addition, the diversity of "types of cruising" is hard to appreciate if you haven't done it, the rivers, the bays, the Gulf, the Ocean, the ICW, the canals, the Great Lakes. Each with its own unique navigational and weather challenges, hazards and beauty, as well as the wide variety of communities from Sabula, Iowa, to Chicago, Illinois and New York City, New York, with all the various people, restaurants, historical sites, scenery, and facilities. What a country! I thought I appreciated the values of America, but this experience raised my gratitude for my life as an American to a completely new level.

Finally, as I continue cruising, even the eighth time down or up the same river, my sense of fulfillment and serenity continues to grow. When a non-boater or even some "dedicated" boaters say, "How can you enjoy that?" or "What do you do all day for 10 (or 14, or whatever) days?" I just smile, because they have no idea; I just plain LOVE IT! And anyone who is with me LOVES IT! That growth is what I've gained from this experience.

Living on the boat all of the time generally wasn't a problem. And, "for the most part" it went fine. I never feel confined on *Souvenir* (with one memorable exception; see Chicago). It's very spacious for its size, with excellent visibility, LOTS of glass and, by the way, ZERO canvas and no "plastic windows"; a real benefit in weather, especially in salt-water. It has six reverse cycle AC/heaters, plus plenty of windows that open, including a huge glass, power sunroof when fresh air is preferred. With the "hard enclosure", there is limited open deck space (no open bridge, and no cockpit; just two sun-pads on the bow). But with our preference for overnights in marinas with power (we only anchor overnight when absolutely necessary), the access to docks, beaches, and courtesy cars provided ample "outdoor time" to offset any inclination to feel constrained to the boat. Plus, our practice of making home visits every couple of months totally refreshed our return to the boat during each segment of the trip. And I felt that the captain and crew coexisted in a very normal and generally healthy environment. We'll see what the crew felt in her addendum!

As previously mentioned, picking a "best" and "worst experience" is very difficult for me. Certainly among the best was our stay in the New York City area during the Fourth of July holiday (docked at Liberty Landing). I achieved one of my dream objectives by circumnavigating Manhattan Island in my own boat, with my family (including son, and daughter's two kids) on the Fourth, then drifting in New York Harbor near the Statue of Liberty that evening to watch four major fireworks displays all around us at the same time. Cruising the Hudson River was another highlight, as well as spending two weeks in Key West, Florida, watching every conceivable type of floating vessel in constant motion while eating a variety of fresh seafood every night. There are many more "bests" too numerous to mention here.

If "worst" is defined as "most challenging," I would list the two rough sea days, one in the Chesapeake Bay, and one on Lake Michigan as the "worst." Defining "worst" as the "least pleasant segment," I would list the Erie Canal (with its lock frequency and speed limit in the blazing heat and humidity of July), and the Illinois River (with its low water, difficulty in getting diesel fuel, and lack of decent marinas that we could access). I would also list our experience in Chicago and Baltimore Harbor as "least pleasant," because of excessive rain. In Baltimore, the disgusting debris washed into the Harbor actually shut down our cooling systems, and the arrogant marina management and staff forced our decision to leave shortly after arrival. We found a delightful alternate marina "up a creek" back near the mouth of the river entering the Chesapeake Bay, and we rented a car to drive into Baltimore to enjoy the amenities. In Chicago over the Labor Day weekend, the constant downpour actually confined us to the boat as if it were a prison, this one-time "confinement" was a problem. However, I view none of those situations as "negatives," but rather just another aspect of the rewarding adventure/challenge/achievement.

If I must pick a "favorite area of the trip," I would have to say Sandestin Golf and Beach Resort, just east of Destin, in the Florida

Panhandle. We loved the place and the people so much that we now call the Resort's Baytowne Marina our "winter homeport," and have spent five winters there on *Souvenir*.

Diane –

The prospect of doing The Great Loop was WAY out of my comfort zone. I grew up near the ocean, love the rivers of Minnesota, and have enjoyed our family boating experiences, but I prefer what has become more familiar. Unlike Dick, "leaving the certainty of our home, and embarking on the unknown" were big issues for me. I agreed to do the Loop with some trepidation primarily because of Dick's passion for it, and I wanted to share it with him. He had spent 37 years totally dedicated to his family and career, and I thought we should do this together, for him, and for us.

A major concern for both of us was my physical limitation due to an almost daily struggle with asthma. So, when *Souvenir* became the comfortable boat that was "meant to be," and we agreed to the basic "rules of engagement" (which included the preference for overnights in marinas with shore power and access to medical facilities, and never cruising at night on purpose), I decided that the risk would be worth the experience.

What I gained from the experience was much like Dick, but in slightly different ways. My sense of accomplishment may have been even greater than his, since the challenges were more of a stretch for me. I think my new perspective and appreciation for our great country and its people has the historical context of the "American Spirit." I found myself constantly fascinated by, and amazed at the image of the pioneers navigating (without aids), crossing the rivers and bays in the wilderness. I reflected on the battles of the Civil War, the lifestyle of the people on the plantations, and the building of the locks and dams, canals, and river towns.

Then, of course, there were the people we met... 99% of them were wonderful, warm, pleasant, happy, helpful, interesting people; and what wonderful memories we have of them all. Just in discussing our input for this book, we enjoyed reminding each other of the dozens of incidents we experienced along every segment of the trip. EVERYONE knows Fern and Hoppie south of St. Louis, Missouri, on the Mississippi River, and Chuck and Barbara in Columbus, Mississippi, on the Tennessee-Tombigbee Waterway. There was the taxi-van driver in Apalachicola,

Florida who gave us an impromptu two-hour guided historical tour of the town with our dog, and only charged us 10 bucks. Then there was the woman running the mom-and-pop marina somewhere along the ICW in the Carolinas. She was a very friendly person selling fuel for 99 cents/gallon, but when she got a radio call from a sailboat going by, she said, "I'm not hauling my fuel hose all the way out on the dock to sell three or four gallons." We also fondly remember the local boating couple in St. Catherine, Ontario, at the lower end of the Welland Canal, who loaned us their car to go to a restaurant for the best Italian dinner we ever had. Then of course, there were the other Loopers and local boaters we met along the way; some we traveled with for several days, a few more than once, and have become life-long friends with several. The list is practically endless. There isn't another 11-month period in my life when I can count so many wonderful new people memories.

I also thoroughly enjoyed re-connecting with numerous friends from both the recent and very distant past, while we traveled and stopped along the way. It had to have been a couple dozen at least, and some went considerably out of their way to visit us on *Souvenir*. For example, there were boating couples we had met in the Florida Keys and Savannah, Georgia, whom we visited later at their homeports on Long Island and Haverstraw, New York. Then there were very memorable moments visiting friends from before our marriage 40 years ago in Oxford, Maryland; Newark, Delaware; Buffalo, New York and Cleveland, Ohio. Our grand-twins were with us to share those wonderful trips down memory lane. Our visit with them to our nation's capital included a meeting with Norm Coleman, the Senator from Minnesota, whom we knew when he was Mayor of St. Paul, Minnesota. Then there was the young man we ran into who grew up around our homeport marina in Minnesota, who is now the Operations Manager of a huge marina we visited near Detroit, Michigan.

Then in Milwaukee, Wisconsin, we visited a cousin of Dick's father whom I had never met; a retired editor of the Milwaukee Journal. And a young woman we visited in Chicago, Illinois, who was a high school classmate of our son. The trip seemed like a constant stream of unions and reunions.

I also have a lot of trouble picking a best or worst experience or favorite place. There are just too many, but as this is such a common question, I have decided that our Fourth of July week in New York City was outstanding. The reason for my enjoyment was being able to be there under such unusual circumstances with our son, his friends, and our grand-twins. It certainly was a once-in-a-lifetime scenario.

The "most challenging" experience for me clearly was our Gulf Crossing from Apalachicola to Clearwater, Florida, in January. Of course, Dick did all the usual research, planning and preparation. I had heard plenty about this part of the "unknown," and it was daunting for me. Due to the short daylight hours, we had engines running and ready to go at "first light." The weather appeared acceptable from the forecast, and we headed across the bay to Government Cut, the channel to the open Gulf. With precise "local knowledge," we kept the range markers on the port side and approached the channel "hugging the greens."

Dick later decided that the source of his local knowledge must have been the cousin of Bubba the Boat US towboat operator. We buried the props in the shoaling sandbar, and sat for two hours watching fishermen and dolphins passing through cleanly on the red side of the channel, while we waited for a tow.

After being towed clear, and following the tow through the channel right where we were told NOT to go, we assessed no damage done, and decided to continue, even though the last hour into Clearwater, Florida, through the crab pots would be done after sunset. A half hour later, with *Souvenir* at cruise speed on autopilot, the forecasted two to three-foot seas were more like four-plus, and we learned something about "confused seas." Billie Jo, our mellow Golden Retriever was under the helm by Dick's feet with her claws buried in the carpet, and a look of terror in her eyes. I was holding onto railings on both sides of the steps to the bridge, with white knuckles, and I could see the grin of enthrallment on Dick's face. And I yelled the phrase that he has since declared would be the name of our next boat, and of his book of the Great Loop, "Adventure, my ass!" The good news is, we had to slow down for a couple of hours, but then the seas calmed and we safely made it through the crab pots in the dark to our destination.

I loved almost every minute of Dick's adventure! I must close by reiterating how much our Great Loop was enhanced by sharing it with our grand-twins, Paige and Blake, who were 11 at the time. They'd been boating with us since they were 10 days old, and literally lived with us for six years while their mom attended college. They joined us for seven weeks and 1,546 miles from Norfolk to Detroit during June/July. They were excellent crew.

Fort Walton, Florida

Butch & Lynne Rachal - *cA*ISLING
Aiken, South Carolina

We first heard about the Great American Loop from an Annapolis couple that had done it twice in the eighties. After meeting Ron and Eva Stob (authors of the book *Honey, Let's Get a Boat* and originators of the America's Great Loop Cruisers' Association) at the Maryland Trawler Fest, we started to put a plan in motion to set out on the Loop ourselves. There can be no better way to cruise for four seasons than by doing the Loop.

Instead of the repetition the ICW snowbirds encounter during their annual migration south to Florida for the winter, and to points north for the hurricane season, the Loop gives you a new experience in many different areas of the eastern United States almost every day. That was our expectation and hope as we set out, and we weren't disappointed.

We sold our house in Annapolis and moved aboard our boat with the intent of cruising for a few years, and settling in South Carolina when we were finished. Our boat, *Aisling*, is a 1978 44-foot Gulfstar Motor Cruiser. Cruising had been a dream of ours for 15 years before we left the dock for the first time. Since we were in a transitional point in our lives, it didn't seem to us to be such a big step to leave the comforts of our home, family, and friends in Annapolis. The most daunting aspect of cruising full-time, especially as we did it by completely turning our backs on our home, is the fact that your "support system" of friends and neighbors is no longer there for you if you encounter a crisis. Sometimes, this is a lonely feeling. The boating community fills some of that void, but cannot fill it all.

Our first cruise was to Florida for the first winter, then we settled in Beaufort, South Carolina for the following winter aboard the boat, and we started the Loop from there. We primarily traveled on our boat alone. While we invited many friends to join us as their schedules permitted, most found the logistics of trying to meet with a boat underway, with an imprecise schedule, to be too daunting for them. We were joined for several legs by close friends from Chapel Hill, North Carolina, and by Lynne's brother. We love to entertain and could have easily had company for 75% of the trip, instead of the 10 to 15 % we actually experienced. Of course, taking into 15 the companionship of the fellow Loopers we met along the way, we really felt that we weren't traveling alone.

The camaraderie that we experienced with these Loopers was one of the highlights of our trip. Early on, we had some major boat problems and we were really down. We were actually considering abandoning the trip when we encountered a couple on a sailboat in West Point, New York. This was our first contact we had made with any other Loopers, and we spent several days with them, in the Catskills of New York, helping them lower and stow their masts. It's hard to believe that working and helping another boater could lift your spirits as it did for us, but we no longer felt alone and on our own. We traveled off and on with that boat all the way to the Tennessee River, before scheduling differences caused us to split up. We're still in close touch with them and get together whenever we can - with or without our boats. We joined up with other Loopers as we proceeded, and by the time we were in the Georgian Bay, we were part of a regular flotilla.

Aisling is an eight-knot boat. We have two staterooms, two heads, and two showers. It is an extremely comfortable live-aboard cruising boat. There is sufficient storage space that we only have to provision quarterly (not counting lettuce and bananas and such), and that includes our substantial bar requirements. The boat has a full bridge enclosure, so we can stay dry in all kinds of weather although depending upon the season, we can be hot or cold up there. It also has a large sundeck which became the "happy hour" site of choice for our flotilla.

Comments from family and friends: "You guys are soooo awesome,"

- "Man, I wish my wife would let me do that," - "You are so lucky that your wife is willing to uproot herself and live on a boat with you," (comment from males and females) - "Can I come too?" (We said yes, but they didn't) - "You guys have both become 'salty' since you've been cruising." (We think that means at ease on the water and the boat).

My wife and I also became better friends as we spent all this time in close quarters, and depended upon each other during some of our crises, large and small. You cannot live in the close quarters demanded by cruising on a boat without developing a tremendous respect for one another, respect for the other's feelings, their privacy, their skills, etc. Most people don't get the opportunity to do this as their daily lives keep them apart most of the time. We seldom raised our voices to one another while cruising. After all, after you yell, scream, and slam the door, where can you go? You have to make it work. In addition, we NEVER yell at each other during anchoring and docking. Our relationship has been strengthened by our experience.

The main thing we have gained from our Great Loop trip was an appreciation of the great diversity that exists in this country (and Canada), and we're not referring to ethnic diversity, but geographical, historical, and cultural. One of the finest aspects of this trip is that every couple of weeks or so, we encountered a completely different experience, including navigational challenges, historical perspectives, natural beauty, and relationships with those on shore. For example, little did we know about the strategic importance of the Hudson River during the Revolutionary War. It literally divided the Colonies in two. If the British had succeeded in controlling that river, they could have isolated the northern colonies, including Boston, from the rest. A week after entering the Hudson River, we were on the Erie Canal, which is responsible for opening up trade between the New York ports and Chicago, etc. Two weeks later, we were walking around Kingston, Ontario, looking at a war memorial for some general who held off foreign invaders. It was a strange feeling to realize that the foreign invaders were Americans. During that two to three week period, we navigated up one of America's major rivers, the Hudson, negotiated 42 locks, and crossed one of the Great Lakes; Lake Ontario. The entire trip mirrors this scenario.

During a trip like this, you have wonderful experiences every single day. They tend to blend to make it seem like a year of cruising through paradise, but then, on occasion, something's going to go wrong. These stand out in our memories like stalagmites. Our best and worst experiences occurred on the same day.

Against the advice of those who know better, we had taken our boat into Crystal River for several days. As we attempted to leave, at low tide, we struck something hard. It scraped along our keel and created several holes in the bottom of our keel. We were taking on water, and couldn't return to the Crystal River. We had no choice but to take off for Tarpon Springs (43 miles and almost seven hours) the nearest place with both adequate depth and a boat yard; we HOPED the bilge pumps would do their job.

Fortunately, the water was coming in just slower than the bilge pumps moved it out. Our float switches were both damaged in the collision so I had to turn them on and off manually, while my wife ran the bridge and stayed in contact with the outside world. It was a harrowing experience and we were pale as ghosts when we finally arrived at the yard in Tarpon Springs. This stands out as our worst experience of the trip. How could this also be our best experience, you might ask?

Remember our focus on friends and the camaraderie associated with cruising? We were traveling with friends, Chuck and Jayne, aboard *Cea Jay*. We'd been traveling with them, off and on, since Oswego, New York. They stayed with us as best they could as we motored toward Tarpon Springs. They also called our friends, John and Maedell, from *Rascal*, whom we had traveled with off and on since West Point, New York. They had completed their Loop a few weeks prior and were at home near Crystal River, Florida. John and Maedell were at the yard when we arrived, and they took us under their wing. They took us to their home, gave us their car, and gave us the friendship we needed.

We cannot overstate how important their friendship was to us at that time. There is one more important element of that day. As soon as we discovered that we had "hurt our boat," we called Towboat US on the radio for advice. While it turned out that we didn't require direct assistance, they were extremely helpful. The local operator had four boats stationed between Crystal River and Tarpon Springs. He put big pumps in each of his boats so they would be ready to assist us should our pumps fail. He also called us on the half-hour just to reassure us that they had our back. Finally, they met us at the entrance to the river and led us right to the boat yard sling. Oh yeah, I forgot. They also called the boat yard and had them on the ready. The staff there delayed their lunch until *Aisling* was safe in their sling. All in all, this was an inspiring experience. Thank the Lord for good friends and good Samaritans!

There are so many wonderfully diverse cruising areas in the Loop. The area we enjoyed the most was the Trent-Severn Waterway. Reasons are – 1: The Canadians were wonderful hosts. 2: As the timing worked out, this was the most relaxing and peaceful part of the trip. Although the locks are a bit of a pain, we enjoyed being able to tie up at night for practically nothing, and visit with friends and locals. The rest of the time we seemed to always be in a hurry or dealing with a problem.

Having said this, we loved every location we cruised for its uniqueness, with one notable exception. WE HATE THE DELAWARE BAY!

Bradenton, Florida

Mary Ellen Mangile - *J*NDIGO *L*ADY
Amherstburg, Ontario

These are four of the most popular questions people asked me during my 5,400-mile, single-handed cruise of the America's Great Loop, in my 20-four-foot sailboat, named *Indigo Lady*. I hope you enjoy them as much as I enjoyed answering them.

WHY? Very often on my trip, people would ask me why I was doing America's Great Loop single-handed. It didn't seem to matter what my answer was; many would have that little glint in their eye and inflection in their tone that said, "You must be crazy." They would nod their head politely, as if to understand when I would try to explain how I wanted to challenge myself. Then, they'd say almost patronizingly, "You certainly are adventurous."

Well, for the rest of the trip anytime someone said I was adventurous, I pretty much figured they were politely telling me I was crazy, and it always made me chuckle a little. Sometimes, I even had to agree with them. I guess you have to be a little curious as to why a woman would take on this kind of challenge by herself.

DON'T YOU GET LONELY? Hmmm… is this a trick question? If I answer "NO," is that bad? If I answer "YES," will the response be, "Then go home?" How should I answer this one? Do they want me to be lonely? I guess it would be normal to admit I was lonely, but then what? Do they expect me to be moping around all the time instead of having the great time I am having? Should I feel guilty for enjoying myself? I don't think so. As it turned out, I answered honestly.

If by lonely you mean do I miss my family? Of course I do. I talk with them almost every day.

If by lonely you mean because I am on the boat by myself and traveling alone, then the answer is definitely "NO". I enjoy being alone with my thoughts and if and when I want company, I just pull into a marina and visit and talk with all sorts of people, just like you."

HAVE YOU HIT ANY BAD WEATHER? For half of my trip, I was quite comfortable and proud to answer "NO". I always explained how I would pay careful attention to the weather reports and not go out when the weather was expected to be less than favorable.

"For the most part, I am a fair weather sailor, but not queasy if I judge it wrong and end up in some foul weather. I certainly don't look for trouble and always wear my life jacket."

That was all well and good for me to say, but somehow I got the feeling that the people who were asking were quite disappointed to hear that I didn't have any exciting weather stories to tell them.

It's a shame I didn't get to meet up with those same people further down the road when I was in the Alligator River in North Carolina, bouncing off a waterspout. Where were they when I had to get out the snow shovel at the end of the Erie Canal in Lockport, New York, on Friday the 13th? Better yet, I could have used a mechanic when my motor conked out in six to eight-foot waves in Lake Erie, and my sail was half draped across my cabin top, having fallen out of the track on the mast. Sure could have told them some bad weather stories then.

WERE YOU EVER SCARED? "You mean besides the nightmare on the Alligator River, and the storm on Lake Erie? Only every time I left the dock!"

Getting back to the little bit of crazy idea, your sanity could be in question when you are willing to leave a perfectly good anchorage or marina slip to head out into the unknown by yourself. I started every day with new butterflies, never knowing what was around the bend. That was the excitement of it though; the little adrenaline rush as I backed out of my slip, the anticipation of something happening and wondering how I would handle it, and then being thankful at the end of the day that nothing had happened.

When I first started on my trip, I noticed the appearance of the other women, who were traveling with their partners. I wondered how they could look so fresh when they arrived at dock at the end of the day; yet I looked like a wilted flower in the middle of the desert. I finally realized that being alone meant so much more than just not having company.

When you are alone, you don't have the luxury of relying on anyone else to help, physically or mentally. It is more than just double the work of a couple; more like 10 times the work. Every decision is yours, every problem is yours to solve, every physical task that needs attention is yours to handle. So many times, I wished I could say, "Honey, could you please hand me up…" or "Honey, could you put the fenders out for me?" Or when I was aground or lost the battle with a crab pot. It's times like that when I would miss having someone with me, for sure. It was exhausting, but overall, I enjoyed being alone.

My solo Great Loop trip was such a learning experience. It was a test of my resolve and a celebration because I had learned to trust myself to get out of the fixes I found myself in. I loved having the satisfaction at the end of the day of thinking to myself, good for you, another day conquered. Most of all at the end of the trip, I loved being able to say, "I DID IT!"

St. Lucie River, Florida

Bill & Betty Bertrand - *Betty B* II
Tullahoma, Tennessee

Friday, December 8th –
We are pulling out of the marina in Columbus, Mississippi, and the friends on a boat that we knew helped us with our lines. It is very cold and the wind has not picked up yet but we expect it to today.

We are very close to the lock that is just south of Columbus, and we will pull in with no problem. We tied the line to the bollard and took the end of the line into the cabin of the boat, because it is too cold outside to stand. On some of the lock doors, we can see icicles hanging down but it does not stop the birds on the top of the lock from looking down at us in the wind-filled lock. There are blue herons and seagulls, like the ones in the Kroger parking lot at home in Tennessee. I guess they think, "What are you crazy people doing out here in the cold?" The birds are so much fun to watch as they fly down into the lock to try to catch a fish, or maybe not. The river is the same south of Columbus as it has been in prior days, with the trees all dead and not much happening today except the barges going up and down the river.

It took us from 8:15 a.m. until 12:20 p.m. to get to this very small, out of the way marina, where we had to negotiate through the red and green markers all the way back into the marina. We were following the greens on the channel and I thought of them as Christmas trees, which made it easier for me to drive. I was driving and the water was deep, at least nine feet, which is good for us because we have a four-foot draft.

The dock was easy to pull into; Bill put out the lines, we got off the boat and walked up the uneven dock that had a four-wheeler sitting on one side of it. There was a houseboat as well, and we think someone once lived in it, along with a sailboat from Florida with no one inside that we could see. The whole place looked deserted, but we went up to the office anyway and found no one there, so we went back to the boat and plugged in the electric cords and just chilled for the afternoon. Oh, one thing, on the way back to our boat, we noticed on a side of the dock the owner had a busted water line from the night before.

The weather here is cold and it is very unusual for this time of year, the locals say. After an hour or so, the owner came back and Bill went to pay for the night's dockage. It gets dark so early that there is not a lot to do outside, and it was such an out-of-the-way place, we only stayed for the one night. So, we read and listened to the Christmas CDs we have. I guess Bill is reading his fortieth book so far on the trip, and I am reading the Jan Karon, Milford series that my girlfriend Suzanne, in Florida, gave me for my birthday last year. I am getting ready to start on the fourth book, which is a very wonderful read about a priest in the small town of Milford.

I have a lot of my Christmas cards mailed out and then when we get the Internet again, I am going to send an e-card as well. I guess that is the thing of the future, or is it now?

So as the sun was going down, it was not completely dark but close, we heard a boat pulling into the small marina, a big 50-footer. It pulled into the slip next to us so we went out to help catch their lines. They were delivering the boat to Tampa, Florida, from Knoxville, Tennessee, so they had had a long day. However, they did not come from Knoxville today, that is just where they picked the boat up.

We could only get some of our phone calls, but the captain of the 50-footer couldn't get any. He asked if he could use our phone and when he did, he had better reception because his boat was much higher than ours was, and therefore the phone worked for him. He wanted to pay us but we said, "No, no that is not necessary." They left very early the next morning and I am sure he runs a lot faster than us, so he probably went to Demopolis, Alabama and it will take us two days to make the same distance. We watched a movie and then went to bed, not a lot of TV here and no Internet, and cell phone reception was spotty, but I am making it just fine.

Saturday, December 9th –
Today, we are going to Sumter Landing on the Tennessee-Tombigbee Waterway. This stop will be an anchorage, and we will have our first night without shore power, but we will have the generator to run so we won't be without heat. We will not run it all night, so we hope it does not get too cold.

We traveled down the river and it was cold so we drove from inside, however, we turned the generator on so we could run our heater and stay warm. It was nice to look out the window and not have coats on.

We traveled for seven-and-a-half hours and arrived around 12:25 p.m. to a very nice Army Corps of Engineers Park. We pulled off the river towards the park and we had to stay in the middle of the entrance of the channel. The park had a launch ramp, picnic tables, and I am sure in the summertime this place is very crowded, but on the December day we're here, there are just two cars. However, the day warmed up enough to sit on top of the boat and read. Once we arrived, we put a line on a dead tree and Bill got into the dinghy and rowed to the other side to tie the stern line to a tree on the shore. I guess we will not go anywhere tonight, and I just hope no other boats come on the other side of us. But it was OK as the other side was very shallow and we did not see anyone all afternoon, except one duck, and a blue heron in a tree that looked around at us for a while. It got real cool when the sun went down so we went inside and started the generator so we could warm the boat up inside before we turned it off for the night.

I'm not sure if I told you all that I did get an electric blanket and it is great, the bed is a queen size, but the way it is shaped I just got a double size and it works great. Only problem is that it did not take long for it to cool off once the generator was turned off.

We were fine until about 5 a.m. when Bill tried to turn the generator on so we could run the heater, however, the sea strainer was full of grass so we had to tough it out until daylight. It was too cold to clean the strainer and it is hard to get at, as it is under the back deck. So, Bill came back to bed and we waited until daylight when he was able to see while cleaning the green grass from the sea strainer. It worked just fine after. You know, when we are home, we do not think of what other boaters are doing when not staying at marinas, it is a whole new world for me as I prefer the comforts of being docked at a marina. I have sure learned a lot over the past 15 months, of course I am a marina girl, you can say that the beauty and the quiet of this river and a good anchorage are nice, but I hope when we come back it is not so cold.

On the rivers, we see so many towboats and they are working 24 hours a day hauling coal, wood shavings, as well as the ones hauling benzene. Of course, on the tows hauling benzene, you see warnings with signs so you know what is in the barge. This week, we saw a tow named Bobby Joe James and, of course, Bill's brother is a Bobby Joe. Being a towboat worker is hard work, and they work so many days on before they get any time off. It's very dirty work, but they help us get our supplies up and down the rivers.

Sunday, December 10th –
Of course, we are up early to get warm and have hot oatmeal and hot chocolate before we ship off. We have the lines untied and Bill had the dinghy back in place on the swim platform.

We are headed to Demopolis Alabama today, traveling down river, and on this stretch we'll see some very unusual rock formations on the side of the river, called Eppes that get even more dramatic as we get closer to them. The rocks are beautiful, they are as big as the ones on the way up to Sewanee, but not brown, they're white. Along the river, there are sandy beaches just like in Florida; it is a beautiful part of our travels. We also go under the U.S. 11 Bridge that parallels I-20 and I-59, the roads that connect Alabama towns to Mississippi towns. We are now exactly half-way between the Tennessee River and downtown Mobile. In Demopolis, we will be leaving the Tennessee-Tombigbee Waterway and entering Black Warrior River.

Demopolis is a good place for Loopers to stop and spend some time. Many go to the store for provisions in preparation for the final days on the river, before arriving in Mobile. We have a friend staying in Demopolis that we traveled with this past summer, his name is Wayne. We saw his boat at the marina we were checking into, but we were not sure if he has gone home to Texas or not. After we checked in, we went to Wayne's boat, he was there, and we had a nice visit. We came down the river system with Wayne; he is single-handing his boat and has just finished the Loop this past summer. We visited Wayne and then he took us to Wal-Mart, then we went to Sonic to eat a burger and drink a diet coke. This is an interesting place in that this is where the towboats fill up, and I guess they have to go to Wal-Mart too. This is where Bobby Joe James was when we pulled in, but before 9 p.m., he was out and on the river again.

We had a beautiful Sunday on the river, enjoying the creation that God made for us.

I know it is hard for you all to realize that we have met so many people, we are so blessed to have made so many friends on this trip that we are still in touch with, and it is like old home week when we cross each other's paths again.

Off to bed now, it will be a long day tomorrow.

Monday, December 11th –
Well, up and out at 6:35 a.m., the earliest morning in a while. It was so nice in the bed, I went back to it after we shipped off, and I stayed until we came to the first lock. It is in Demopolis so I was not there long, but I did get up and put my life jacket on, and Bill did the lines outside. I did not want to scare the lockmaster with this wild crazy morning looking person. So I just decided to go back to bed and Bill drove from inside and I was just there sleeping until 8:45 a.m. By then it had warmed up enough outside, I got up and we went topside to drive on the flybridge.

This is a beautiful day and they say it is going to get warm, up into the sixties, so this will be good. Today we will go almost 70 miles to an anchorage along the side of the river. As it turned out it was a great day and I drove for about three hours while Bill read. I know, can you believe it; I did have to put shorts and a sleeveless tee shirt on, because it was so warm. It was so interesting to see how the river changed during the day, some of it is very clear down through the water, and some has sand, it would be fun to drive the ski boat up on the sand and have a picnic, but not today.

Today, we made it to Bashi Creek, an anchorage back off the river beside another park. We pulled off the main part of the river and put the bow anchor out, then we added a stern anchor so we would not move around during the night. We sat on the top of the boat and just read, and of course, I listened to the birds sing to one another. This was a beautiful place. We sat outside until almost dark and then went inside.

One good thing about traveling at this time of year, we have no bugs. So, we had a spaghetti dinner tonight and then our usual, but Bill went out to check the boat and turn off the generator. He said, "You have to see the stars." It was wonderful how many thousands there were, and they were all so white, and you could see so many from where we were in this small deep cove. No one came around, of course, who would in the cold winter except the towboats. They would come around a turn in the river, I would look out, and it looked like a hotel passing by with all the lights on in the boat, and pushing the load up and down the river. It was a little scary to see it so close, but we knew it could not get to where we were. But the night was great and the stars looked like you could pick them from the sky.

Tuesday, December 12th –
We had a great night, it was not too cold and it was a great sleeping night. Bill started the generator about 6 a.m. and we were going to leave today to go to Bobby's Fish Camp. Bobby's is the only dock on the river from here to Mobile, but it is just a dock with no electric, but they do have fish cabins, a store, and a restaurant. The restaurant is just open Thursday through Sunday, and we're stopping on a Tuesday so no catfish for us. They say the catfish is great, but we will see when we come back through in the spring.

We will anchor out through Thursday night, as the anchorages are great because it is so calm and the locations are off the river, up an inlet, or in a creek. We set both the anchors even though there is no tide, because we wanted to remain in one position all night.

While we were underway, I cleaned and rearranged our supplies, pots, and pans. We have storage under the guest bed so I am using one side for extra supplies. I think that this will work out better for our galley storage. I do not know why I told you all this but we just have to make the best of what we do with our storage. Along the river today, we passed a lot of summer fishing cabins on stilts. They are on stilts as this area floods and they have to be built up high.

Tonight, we are on our way to Bates Lake; it is not a large place but a good place to anchor, and we were not disappointed. We sat on the back of the boat when we finished getting the anchors set, and just enjoyed the quiet. Another quiet night and the fog came in early so we did not see too many stars.

Thursday, December 14th
This morning, we were fogged in and it was so thick you could not see but the front of the boat. We decided to stay put for a while and watch TV this morning, and just enjoy the time to sit. We did pull anchor, and go out in the river, as Bill was thinking the fog was not too bad out there, but we came back and dropped the anchor again. We both just read and waited until 11 a.m.

As we were driving along, Bill would give me information out of our cruising guide. We went by Lovers Leap, a rare bit of fine scenery along this stretch, cracked, and colored rock, trees with gnarled roots clinging to the cliff and wisps of Spanish moss make it easy for watching. This is one bit of trivia about the Spanish moss. It is neither a true moss nor a parasite. It's a member of the pineapple family, and survives by absorbing water from the air. We also passed so many cypress trees, the Spanish moss, marsh grass, and so many birds on the side of the river.

Our anchorage tonight was at the Tensaw River Cut-off Channel, and this is one of the great hurricane holes that local boaters use to seek safety when the big storms come in. From here we turned onto Big Briar Creek, which is a nice area about 300 feet wide, so we have a good place to anchor for the night.

Friday, December 15th –
Again today, we get up to fog, and had to wait until the fog lifted, which was around 11:30 a.m. We pulled up the anchor and then got on our way to Mobile. It was a quiet trip until we got to the shipyards at the mouth of Mobile Bay.

There were huge boats on both sides of the river, and very large buildings. We saw two ships that the U.S. Coast Guard has fire drills on to practice on putting out boat fires. This is busy place, with a lot of tugs pushing and pulling barges. We had to look a lot on both sides of the river to see what was happening.

After we came out through the ship yards, we were in fog on Mobile Bay so we followed a towboat for a while until we got our bearings, and then we passed the tow while using our radar to help us navigate through the thick, white fog.

After about an hour, the wind blew and cleared the fog out, this was about 2 p.m. We finally made it into the Dog River Marina in Mobile and we will have the boat here until end of December, as we are flying out to California to see Bridget and Matt for Christmas. We will then fly back to Mobile, then head around the coast of Florida and finish the Loop sometime in January. We are looking forward to the friends and family we will see in Florida.

We are getting excited about the finish, and it is so hard to believe that we have gone all the way around the Loop, a 7,200-mile adventure.

New Smyrna, Florida

Dick & Carol Masse - ᒿANOPUS
St. Leonard, Maryland

We took the Great Loop boat trip because we felt it would be an adventure of a most unusual nature. We had been thinking about it for a while, as we had made other types of trips around the United States, specifically the East Coast, and visited some of the ICW areas. These experiences gave us the initial idea of traveling by boat, which then grew into the Great Loop trip. We decided that it would be exciting, adventurous, and just plain fun! We didn't think leaving the comforts of home really entered into the equation to a large degree. We wanted to do it now as we felt health issues, or other issues might preclude us from doing it later. It truly was an unknown, but we felt we would be competent enough to handle it, and even though Carol didn't have any boating experience to speak of, she was wholeheartedly supportive of the trip.

We elected to take a multiyear approach to doing the Loop after reading the AGLCA's newsletter articles, and talking with people who had already completed it. Many felt that they had accomplished the trip in too short a time. That theme seemed to be prevalent in many of the discussions we had with people, and the idea of a multiyear event would be more satisfying for us. With a longer time frame we felt we could do the trip justice. What that means is we could spend all the time we desired in those places that held more interest to us, for whatever reason. Our mantra became: "Await occasions, hurry never." And we didn't. Our average day started at 10-11 a.m. and ended at 3 p.m. or so. We took five years to complete the Loop, with stops at, in order: Kingston, Ontario; Chicago, Illinois; Chattanooga, Tennessee; and Mobile, Alabama. We put the boat up each year and winterized her.

Canopus is a double cabin with a stateroom down aft and a V-berth down and forward. We have the usual items of comfort, although in miniature of course; refrigerator, microwave, four-burner stove, etc. The command bridge is completely covered, and so we spend all of our time underway up there, unless the weather is atrocious. We slept aft while guests used the V-berth. When kids were aboard, we lowered the galley table and made room for them.

Our trip plans started approximately one year in advance of the journey, with both of us taking courses with the Coast Guard and the U.S. Power Squadron. We took courses in safety, marine electronics, piloting, advanced piloting, CPR, seamanship, and cruise planning. We discussed many things in advance, especially what kind of clothes to bring, types of tools, spare parts, meal planning, safety issues, and first aid stuff to name a few things.

We learned many new things. We wanted to see America from a very different perspective than the one we'd always had. We'd done a lot of traveling throughout the country, but never in this way. We wanted to relearn our history and felt this would be a way to accomplish that. We were right. The biggest thing we have gained is a greater appreciation of our country, its history and roots, and how bits and pieces of history fit together in a quilt work of development across the country, and the settlement of different areas. It led to knowing more about the industrial movement, the War of 1812, the Civil War, and many other things, too numerous to mention. The other lesson it taught us was how simply one can live when you are on a boat. It was wonderful!

Living on the boat for the most part was a joy! Because we were living on the boat, we feel we were much more tolerant of each other than perhaps we would have been had we been ashore. There were a couple of times when we thought we shouldn't do it, but that was when we were still close to home! After we got away from home a bit, we settled in for the long haul and simply made it work without too much difficulty. We learned to appreciate each others strengths and tolerate each others weaknesses and a sense of humor always helped.

Renting cars, touring with our bikes, hitchhiking, and hiking away from the boat all enhanced our trip. We would sometimes take bike trips in excess of 45 miles. We found the added range these methods provided us heightened our travel experience, and made for some enjoyable moments, which is another story in itself, like the heart specialist sailor who picked us up and gave Carol free meds!

We did the trip by ourselves for most of the way, with friends and family joining us for brief periods. The longest visit, from a pregnant daughter, lasted about 10 days. This visit turned out to be valuable for her as it allowed a bad pregnancy to become much more manageable, even though she fell in the engine room on her first day! Because our boat is small, 34 feet, our feeling was a visit of more than one week could be quite challenging unless it was with very close family. And then, of course, you are supposed to tolerate almost anything!

We had visitors on each leg of the journey, with a couple of daughters visiting while in Florida. The most we ever had on board was eight; four children and four adults sharing the boat. It was a bit tight. Our youngest guest was four and the oldest was 93!

Our attitude was always one of excitement and expectation when expecting guests, and this feeling continued while they were there. We became very open about inviting people we cared about to join us at any time of their choosing, and we never turned anyone away! Maybe we wanted them to see how we were managing the trip, and gain some experience on the boat with us as well. We didn't feel people really understood the nature of what it was that we were doing. They didn't appreciate the trials and tribulations that go along with this type of a trip. Part of our intent was to demonstrate to them what it was all about so, we spent a lot of time educating our guests on the boating experience, and discussed such things as buoys, beacons, navigation aids, boat handling, weather, locking through, etc.

As far as what our family and friends thought or felt, some said we were nuts, others asked why we would do it, but mostly, others said it would be neat and a great idea. There were those who felt it was one of those dreams one should fulfill. Mostly, we received positive reviews and good wishes, although the older members of the family did show a little concern.

Our trip was 8,620 miles because we did several things differently from the other Loopers. Our route took us from Maryland to the Hudson River, then into Canada via Lake Champlain to Montreal, Ottawa, and then to Kingston, where we learned of 911. We could go no further than that, so we put the boat on the hard in Kingston, Ontario, and came home, planning to rejoin her in the early spring.

Year two consisted of heading east around Lake Ontario, then into the Erie Canal and all the way back to Troy, New York. We continued out at Oswego to Buffalo, New York, St. Catherine and Toronto, Ontario and eventually into the Trent-Severn Waterway. We cruised up to Sault St. Marie, then into Lake Michigan, hugging the north shore down to Green Bay, Wisconsin, and then heading south on the west side of the lake to Chicago, Illinois. We put her up again and came home.

Year three was from Chicago to the Illinois River up the Mississippi River to La Crosse, Wisconsin, then back down the mighty river to the Ohio River. Then it was on to the Cumberland River all the way up, a few miles shy, and back down to the Tennessee River. We went all of the way up the river to Knoxville, Tennessee and checked out the Little Tennessee, then back down to Chattanooga, Tennessee, for the winter.

Year four consisted of doing the Tennessee River down to the Tennessee-Tombigbee Waterway and on to Mobile, Alabama, where we left the boat during the hurricane season. We almost lost her to Ivan, but things turned out OK. The boat fell off the jack stands when they broke while we were at home, but they were good at making the repairs, etc. required. Not too much damage really. Again, we felt lucky!

Year five had us leaving Mobile, Alabama, and doing the northern route of Florida to St. Marks, Steinhatchee, Cedar Key, Tarpon Springs, etc. Quite a jaunt that was, as it was the first time we had encountered fog, shallow water and, of course, stone crab traps! Then on to Stuart, Florida via Lake Okeechobee up to Jacksonville, and a side trip up the St. Johns River. Then it was the ICW back to Maryland, arriving and completing our Great Loop Adventure.

Oyster Creek - St. Augustine, Florida

Erica Northwood & Kevin Burns - $\mathcal{K}$ISMET III
Niagara Falls, Ontario

We completed the trip with three of us aboard. Kevin the Captain, Erica the Admiral, and our family dog Luci (a yellow Lab-Boxer mix) formed our crew. Erica and I had only been together just over a year when we embarked on the trip. We weren't sure that we could survive living 24/7 in such a small space, and we weren't sure how Luci would handle it either.

Here we are, a year later, with 5,400-plus miles under our keel, and we are more in love now than when we started. Oh, and Luci? She loves the boat and has enjoyed the trip immensely, especially since she guarded us against all manner of creatures (especially those dangerous dolphins!) that constantly threatened us.

We bought a project boat, a 1976 43-foot Viking Motor Yacht. She has two cabins, two heads, full galley, saloon, dinette and two steering stations. She has twin Detroit Diesel engines and a full 8-kW generator. We started the trip without a canvas enclosure, thinking that it wasn't necessary. About 10 days into the trip, a full canvas enclosure was raised to the top of the improvement priority list. *Kismet III* is a Canadian flagged boat, and she is a loving work-in-progress. She has been the perfect Looper boat for us.

Erica and I each had been boaters in our previous lives, so we knew we wanted to continue this lifestyle together. We heard about the Loop from some fellow boaters in Georgian Bay, Ontario. We decided to investigate and see if it made sense for us. Our research on the AGLCA website lasted about three hours and looked intriguing, so we decided to go for it, but soon we recognized the need for a larger and more Loop-efficient boat, as the Bayliner we owned, in Georgian Bay, was much smaller and was gasoline powered. Fortunately, we found *Kismet III* in Florida, and we decided she was the perfect boat for the Loop.

We spent about four months in Fort Lauderdale, Florida, making some repairs on the new boat. We read some Skipper Bob books and bought the necessary charts. Then we jumped on board and went! While many Loopers have lots of toys on board, such as fancy chart plotters and auto helm systems, we decided to go bare bones on electronic equipment. We did the Loop trip with just a hand-held GPS, a compass, and a depth sounder. Talk about a learning curve! Tides, currents, freighters, barges, and open ocean boating were all new to us, not to mention diesel engines and a boat with infinitely more systems than our former small Bayliner on Georgian Bay.

We traveled back to Canada at least a half dozen times during the journey. We wanted to visit with family and friends, so they didn't think that pirates had captured us!

We hoped to gain a number of things by completing the Loop. We hoped to reaffirm our love of boating and of living aboard. In the past year and one week, we have been with each other 24/7 in a small space with a large dog, experiencing all sorts of things that are new to us. The trip has been an awesome journey and we most definitely have confirmed that we love boating, we love living aboard, and we love each other more now than before the trip. Our goal (and dream) is to continue living aboard for as long as we can and cruise to other countries to enhance our experience even more.

Living on the boat for this period has been a series of learning curves unknown to those who live on land. Erica and I prefer the solitude and surrounding nature of anchoring to tying up in a marina, so we had to learn to cope with the weather. A wonderfully tranquil anchorage can become a rolling nightmare in high winds. We had to learn to take what we get in terms of weather, and just live with it.

We learned to be a lot more self-sufficient in terms of provisioning. Finding the basics like ice and water was a problem, especially if we didn't plan well. Similarly, finding a pump out was challenging at times, which required vigilance and planning to avoid a messy experience. Since there are very few 7-Elevens handy on the ICW, we learned the value of forward planning so that fairly basic items could be obtained without a lot of inconvenience; something those on land don't always need to be concerned with.

There is no question that we went through some "bumpy" times on the trip, but we learned, as boaters on the move, that you can control very few things, and must roll with the flow. Our relationship is stronger because of this trip; we have reaffirmed our commitment to each other, to boating, and to living aboard. All things considered, our experience has been very positive and we are pleased that the Loop has been everything (and more) that we hoped it would be.

For us, there were few bad experiences, but in retrospect, being on a "schedule" to fly home to deal with business was a problem at times. Because we generally flew back to Canada (as opposed to driving a rental car), we had to schedule ourselves to be in a relatively large city to book our flight. As a result, this caused us added stress as we had to rush through part of the journey, not being able to stop and enjoy, as we would have liked. Since we don't plan to do the Loop again, we may have missed out on some wonderful experiences that are now lost forever.

There are so many great experiences; it's hard to narrow it down. Having said that, Erica and I agree that our single best experience of all along the trip has been a profound appreciation for life and nature. The world is such a huge and awesome place, and the plants and animals we have encountered have been absolutely fantastic. Seeing dolphins and manatees around the boat was especially amazing.

Erica and I agree that the Erie Canal was our favorite area on this trip. We could finally leave tides and currents behind us for a while, and enjoy many small towns, like Waterford and Oswego, while transiting 27 locks before reaching Lake Ontario. However, the real joy for us on the Erie Canal came in the form of a young Canada goose. She swam past our boat, came out on land, and planted herself in a water puddle not far from us. When we approached her for a closer look, Erica noticed she had fishing line twisted around her neck, and a fishing hook embedded in the back of her neck. The poor bird couldn't eat or drink properly and we were afraid that she had been abandoned by her flock and would die. We managed to remove the fishing line and hook, and were so relieved to see her stretch her neck and immediately begin to eat and drink. As we were leaving the lock a few days later, we saw her with the rest of the flock as they prepared for the long migration. It warmed our hearts to know that we had had an opportunity to give something back to nature. What a special moment for us, one that we will remember for a lifetime.

The people along this part of the journey were extraordinary. The lock staff was very friendly and accommodating. During the flooding of the Erie Canal, we were asked by many locals if we were OK or if we needed anything. One fellow even drove us to a Home Depot so that we could get some materials to fix our boat. Another highlight of the trip was coming into New York harbor, and seeing Lady Liberty from the water not more than 500 yards from our boat, a truly awe-inspiring sight, especially since we could anchor for the night right behind her. One of the highlights of the last leg of the river-system adventure was meeting the colorful characters at "Hoppie's Marina," on the Mississippi, and "Bobby's Fish Camp," on the Tennessee-Tombigbee Waterway. These marinas were little more than a barge tied to shore in the first case, and a dock (I use that term very loosely here) tied to shore in the second case, but they were manned by very colorful locals who added a nice bit of local flavor to our trip.

We crossed our wake at the St. Lucie Inlet (mile marker 988 on the Intracoastal Waterway) about 88 miles north of Fort Lauderdale. We dropped a hook in nearby Peck Lake to toast the closing of our Loop. As Captain Kevin popped the cork on the champagne bottle, and First Mate Luci happily slugged on her bowl of water, Admiral Erica brought out some pictures and we began to reminisce about the great, the bad, and the ugly of our Loop journey. Some people spend months, even years, planning a trip like this. We spent one year and one week completing a journey that we researched for only a few hours. And we loved every minute of it.

We have come to realize that this trip has been nothing short of amazing. The world truly is a big, wonderful place, full of all sorts of nature, which never failed to amaze us. We are blessed to have each other, and good friends and family who have supported us in this adventure. We have reaffirmed our love of boating, and our desire to continue to live aboard for as long as we can. It's been one heck of a ride!

Savannah, Georgia

Jeremy Bell & Janet Crane - TARDIS
Green Cove Springs, Florida

Janet –

My husband, Jeremy, and I completed our Great Loop trip on our boat *Tardis*. She is a 34-foot American Tug, and she has proven to be a capable and comfortable floating home over the past year. We had owned a 34-foot sailboat and wanted something about the same size, but a trawler rather than a sailboat. Having previously cruised extensively on our sailboat, we learned that we very rarely sailed when traveling. Since we were most often really a powerboat masquerading in a sailboat's clothing, we decided it would make sense to give up the pretense and go over to the dark side of a powerboat. We love the fact that our American Tug draws only three-and-a-half feet (versus the five-and-a-half feet of our sailboat), plus we can reduce the air draft down to only 13 feet (versus 55 feet with our sailboat). We are happy to report that with our new "streamlined" dimensions, we have touched the bottom far fewer times and are able to slide gracefully under most of the bridges that we have come across. She is powered by a single diesel, which, together with the bow thruster (which I've named Thomas – the little thruster that could), is reasonably easy to manage between the two of us.

We purchased *Tardis* on the West Coast, in Seattle, Washington. We spent a few months the first summer we had her cruising in the beautiful San Juan and Golf Islands, before taking her down the coast to our home in Alameda, a small island city near Oakland, California in the San Francisco Bay. Last year, we sold our house, moved onto *Tardis*, and trucked her to the East Coast so that we could do the Great Loop.

The reason we decided to do the Great Loop trip is simply that, we love to travel. We love seeing new places, and meeting new and interesting people. We also really enjoyed the time we spent living on and traveling on our sailboat - so we had always planned on living aboard again one day, and doing some more extensive cruising.

We have several friends with boats who have taken these types of trips in the past. These friends were extremely supportive and encouraging of our plans. Most of our other friends thought we were crazy, but were supportive and wished us well. Family is a whole other matter. My mom thinks we are insane, and continues to wonder when we will give up this 'foolishness' and settle down as dependable members of the family.

Cruising in a small boat has given us a stronger sense of self-reliance and confidence. I can now report that while I still can't parallel park a car, I can successfully parallel park a 34-foot powerboat!

Living together on the boat is great - but then we've done it before on a sailboat, and we didn't kill each other that time, so I figured it would probably be a safe bet that we wouldn't kill each other this time either.

We've had many wonderful experiences since we've been cruising on our boat. Probably the most thrilling was passing by the Statue of Liberty on our boat in New York harbor. The worst experience for me was probably the night we spent anchored in the Ohio River, with a strong current sending logs and branches past our boat. Still, we weren't hit by anything large, so it really wasn't that bad. Someone else reported seeing a refrigerator floating past a few days before we got there. Being hit by a fridge on the Ohio - now THAT would count as a bad experience!

Jeremy –

For me, the worst experience was a huge thunderstorm near Fort Frederica, Georgia. Despite dropping the antennas, I thought we might still be hit by lightning. It's the first time I've ever heard a "crack" that loud as the lightning struck extremely close by.

Janet –

Our favorite area was Canada, especially the North Channel and the canals (especially the Rideau and Chambly) for the slow pace and lovely small towns along the way. The North Channel stood out for its rugged, pristine beauty.

Intracoastal Waterway, South Carolina

Sue Hamel & Jim Brown - *Water Dancer* III
Haslett, Michigan

Jim and I are traveling on the Great Loop by ourselves. It's certainly nice to have friends join us along the way, but we feel that the space on the boat is just right for our pets and us. We are traveling with a parakeet, Linus, and a cat, Sneakers. Our pets are good companions, easy to care for and provide entertainment and affection. Linus talks; he's a very happy bird. And Sneakers loves her petting first thing every morning.

Water Dancer III is a very comfortable boat for us. She is a 1987 44-foot Seamaster Motor Yacht powerboat. Her height is 17 feet, draft is 3 feet 7 inches and beam is 13 feet 9 inches, she is a twin diesel with a semi-displacement hull. Our cruising speed is 10 miles per hour although she can max out at 22. She has two staterooms, the master has a queen-size bed, and the forward stateroom has bunk beds, each room has an adjoining head. We have a galley down arrangement with dishwasher, microwave, stove, oven and a dinette opposite the galley. We also have a washer/dryer and lots of room for storage. There is a cockpit, which is very convenient for storing our bicycles, and is invaluable when working lines and locking through.

We enjoy boating and have owned boats of various sizes for years. We started with small powerboats, and enjoyed tubing, water skiing and other water sports. We graduated to larger weekender powerboats. Our previous boat, *Water Dancer II*, was a 29-foot Sea Ray Sundancer.

However, being Michigan boaters and employed, our boating was limited to good weather weekends during only five months of the year, and an occasional week during the summer. Fortunately, we were both able to retire at the same time while we are still relatively young. Our dream was to spend more time boating and traveling. A few years before retiring, we began taking Power Squadron classes, attending Trawler Fests, and learning more about the America's Great Loop Cruisers' Association (AGLCA). We read, *Honey, Let's Get a Boat*, and began to explore the Loop route. Our plan for retirement has always been to move south and to travel. So, the idea of doing this by boat was just another way of experiencing our dream. We also decided that living on a boat would be our retirement lifestyle, negotiable year to year with a possible three to five-year maximum. During our travels, we intend to search for the perfect retirement spot to settle.

Therefore, we sold our home, put our belongings in storage, (including a car), for the time when we would once again become dirt dwellers. So, we still have options open to us and have not cut any ties. We stay in contact with family and friends via phone and e-mail, so we don't feel we left anyone behind.

We bought our boat in St Petersburg, Florida, and kept it in Palmetto, Florida, for a couple months to have it outfitted for our needs. We left Palmetto, came across to the eastern side of Florida, and wintered in the Keys. During the spring, we followed the circle route through the Atlantic ICW, to the Chesapeake Bay, Hudson River, and Erie Canal. We were forced to evacuate our boats in the Erie Canal when it flooded 20 feet over flood level in June of that year.

That experience detained us for six weeks, during which time we met some wonderful local townspeople who cared for us and made our stay pleasant. We then moved on to Canada via the Trent-Severn Waterway route, and through the Georgian Bay and North Channel. We came into the Great Lakes at Drummond Island, Michigan, and journeyed down Lake Michigan along the Michigan shoreline.

Being from Michigan, we spent some extra time in her ports to visit with friends via car, and to have family and friends visit us on the boat. We are currently headed down the river system, and plan to stay for a few weeks in Kentucky and Tennessee, in both places we will be joined by friends for a few days, then on to Florida in December. At that point, we will have completed the Loop. We intend to stay in Florida for the winter, including the Keys, and possibly a trip to the Bahamas. In the spring and summer, we will return to the Chesapeake

Bay before returning to Florida for the following winter.

Responses from our friends and family really do vary. Jim's mother is worried about us; we do find that some people believe this to be a dangerous venture. Many don't seem to understand that we are never far from land or a marina. Others think it's an exciting thing to do, although nothing they would personally attempt. Others envy us because it's a dream that they share, or they are just happy that we can be living our dream. Others are just curious about what we've seen, adventures we've had, and wondering how we do common things like paying bills, shopping, etc. Others wonder about our relationship, and how we can be with each other 24/7. All our family and close friends plan to see us on the boat sometime during our adventures. Some will choose to stay on the boat, others at a nearby land-based hotel. The number of people who follow our adventures surprises us. They visit our website, some we don't even know (friends of friends etc.).

Living on a boat full-time with only your spouse and pets adds a different perspective to your relationship. Gone is the freedom to just leave anytime you want to be alone, see friends, or just take a breather. However, we find that our relationship is very satisfying. Sure, there are moments of stress, but for the most part being with each other has been enjoyable. It takes maturity in a relationship to be together 24/7 in a small space, because you definitely have to learn to be more relaxed and tolerant of each other, and not to sweat the small stuff. We have learned how to give each other the space we need. However, even after all this time together, we still like and enjoy being with one another.

For us, the best and worst experience is one and the same; it was being stuck for almost 15 days on the Erie Canal. It was the worst because of the stress and anxiety during the time of the flood. We were rescued off our boat at six in the morning, and watched the water rise to 20 feet above flood level. The currents rushed past the boat, carrying huge pieces of debris. It left us wondering if we would have a boat to return to. Later, when the crisis was over, we saw the water levels recede too far and it actually grounded our boat. We regret the time we lost that we couldn't make up without missing some of the things we wanted to see and do in Canada and Michigan. On the other hand, it was the best experience because we spent the time with wonderful people, and made some lasting friendships.

A few other bad experiences were: the nasty weather we

encountered on Lake Michigan, and the lower Chesapeake Bay, locking and docking in wicked winds and/or fast currents as we worried about damaging our boat or someone else's boat.

While our favorite places vary between us; Jim says the Florida Keys. He loves the warmth and beauty of the area as well as the relaxed atmosphere. Sue says the big cities: New York, Chicago, Baltimore, Miami, and Norfolk. It is great to be in a marina right downtown, and be able to get off your boat and explore these vibrant cities that offer fine dining, great museums, wonderful shopping, and great sights. We experienced how supportive and helpful people can be during a disaster, and how everyone pulls together.

Other things that stand out as best experiences are: Cruising your own boat into New York Harbor and seeing the Statue of Liberty and the Manhattan skyline; the many lovely, serene anchorages in the Chesapeake and Georgian Bays, coming back to our homeport in Michigan and receiving enthusiastic and heartfelt greetings, and being treated like returning royalty coming back from a great adventure.

We both have gained a greater ability to drive and handle our boat. We have met so many wonderful people, and truly have enjoyed the company of fellow Loopers and other boaters. We have developed greater self-confidence in managing difficult and strange situations. Learning to trust and depend on each other has brought us closer. Although we haven't yet found the perfect place to settle after all of this boat traveling, we still enjoy looking and exploring the country.

Dowry Creek, North Carolina

Jim & Lynda Dunwell - *PATIENCE*
Key West, Florida

As we traveled north on our Great Loop trip, we wanted to visit places that we hadn't seen on our first Loop. So, as we ventured out in the North Carolina waters, we were first attracted to what we had heard about the history of Ocracoke Island. This island was where Blackbeard the pirate made his base, and where he eventually met his fate. It's a low-lying island with a safe harbor at the end of the outer islands of North Carolina. We loved the fact that the National Park service had a dock, and with our Golden Age Pass, we get half off.

The weather is always in the back of our minds, and it was forecast to be 10 to 15 knots, which is the highest that we feel comfortable boating in. It was sunny and beautiful when we ventured out of Ocracoke to cross the Pamlico Sound. Everything was fine for about an hour, and then things quickly took a turn for the worse. Waves rose up to eight to 10 feet, and the winds were gusting up to 40 knots. Needless to say, we had to tack into the wind and gut it out.

Boaters were caught off guard all over the Sound. Later, they were demanding that the Coast Guard revise the forecasts so other people wouldn't be caught in the same situation. We rocked and rolled for a good hour. It was a very uncomfortable situation. It was probably the worst conditions that *Patience* has encountered. We certainly have a new regard for Blackbeard's home area.

We then had to make the choice of going north through the Dismal Swamp route (last year's choice), or a more outside route through a town called Coinjock, North Carolina. The advantage of the Coinjock route is that there is a restaurant on the way that serves a 32-ounce portion of prime rib. The world famous prime rib won out. We ordered just one serving, which we had for lunch and dinner the next day, and still had some left over. Not good for the heart but we were only going to be in Coinjock once.

The outside route was a little quicker, but we were constantly being waked by high waves that we couldn't avoid. Oh, how we hate inconsiderate boaters in large powerboats. We arrived in Norfolk, Virginia, and took a little time out to visit family, and then we drove to a reunion of Lynda's Pi Phi Sorority at Michigan State University.

We left Norfolk (the Navy Base) in early June, heading into the Chesapeake Bay. We worked at going to different ports. Our first was Tangier Island, Virginia. You only get to Tangier by your own boat or by ferry. It is filled with lobstermen and clamers. They have staked out little islands around the harbor, where they built houses on sticks and timbers in the tidal mud. They bring their boats up to little stands, and off-load their crabs and clams into tanks. Once in the tanks, they monitored their cycles until the crabs shed their shells, and while still soft, they are sold. It's quite an operation. We spent two days there and had a great time walking around. Very few cars, mostly golf carts. It's a part of the country you don't get to see, or experience often.

We seemed to hit Baltimore's inner harbor on the hottest day of the year. We were going to anchor but the heat drove us to the dock, where we could run our air conditioning. Our trip down the Delaware Bay went well, as did our trip up the coast of New Jersey. We went outside where we could. Last year, we hit a lot of rough water on this stretch. We tucked in behind Sandy Hook, New Jersey and enjoyed going out to dinner. Now, it's off to the 79th St. anchorage on the Hudson River. We'll pay $30 a night and it's only a quarter-mile to the subway and Times Square. That's a deal every boater should take advantage of.

Lynda had her itinerary and I followed her along. We went to the Museum of Modern Art that afternoon, and then we saw "Beauty and the Beast", the play, that evening. We had tried to get tickets to the "The Jersey Boys" which is the story of Frankie Valli and "The Four Seasons." This play had just won the Tony Award for Best Musical, so it was a long shot. We waited in line as if we were groupies, and by golly, someone returned two tickets and we got in. It has to be the best musical we have ever seen. If you went to college in the sixties, you will love the story and the music.

A strange thing happened that night. I've been known to sleepwalk in my younger days. We were on a mooring buoy on the Hudson, and I must have been worried about its holding ability. Well, I got up and with all the lights of the city, I had the feeling that we were drifting down the river and in harm's way. I saw these huge pilings nearby and feared that we were going to hit them. Quickly, I dashed to the lower helm, started the engines, put them in gear and started to move slowly away. I was a little upset we weren't moving as quickly away from the pilings as I wanted. Guess what, I woke up and found to my amazement that I was still tied up to the mooring ball. I turned off the engine and went back to bed thinking, "Well, that's a story few people will believe." Lynda's comment was, "I heard the engine but I just turned over." Oh well, just don't accept our invitation to sleep aboard and you will be fine.

We left New York City early to catch the tide going through Hell's Gate, which is where the water flows from the East River and hits the Long Island Sound's flow. A decent whirlpool forms, and the current can be three or four knots at full tide. We slid through at slack tide, so presto, we were in the Sound. We stayed on the Long Island side for a couple of days, and then crossed over to Connecticut. We had a delightful run up the Connecticut River and stopped at Essex. We stayed for free at the town docks and met our good friends Diba and Paul and their kids. The next day, we went further up to Deep River and met our HS-74 Navy friends, Larry and Pat.

I must tell you that when you have owned an Inn in the mountains of New Hampshire, you tend to have many friends. We zeroed in on another pair in Watchic Hill, Rhode Island, Lenny and Lorn. OK, then we headed over to Block Island with about a 1,000 other boats on the Fourth of July weekend. I mean it was a real zoo. We were to meet two other guests of ours, Nora and Bill, who would be coming out to meet us in their boat. We were to be the "Mother Ship."

They arrived ahead of us and when we entered the Great Salt Pond, we had to look for them out of thousands of boats. Fortunately, our cell phones worked and we met. Bill had a lovely new boat that he brought alongside a not-so-new but proud *Patience*. If you have ever been to Block Island, you know the drill, dinghy into shore and walk a mile or two to town. I think everyone on the island was younger than us. I started to feel my age when people gave me sidewalk space so I wouldn't wobble into them. One thing I certainly won't forget happened as we were walking into town, a girl came bicycling by us wearing a bikini top and a thong. I dropped and then stepped on my camera amidst all the confusion, meanwhile she was out-distancing my beady eyes. So, it's just a dream now. One that I hold dear in my heart.

Now, there we were walking back to our dinghy on the shore, one-and one-half miles (and I was still hyperventilating over the thong thing), we noticed the tide had gone out quite a bit.

Well, lo and behold, as we motored around the corner, I noticed that *Patience* was lying very still in three feet of water. Well, I needed at least four feet. So I guess you could say we were hard aground. After a quick inspection. I declared, "no harm, no foul." We decided to wait until high tide and then have Sea Tow pull us free. Now, the Sea Tow operators, over the past four years, have become very good friends of ours. Whenever we hit a sandbar (uncharted) etc., we would call Sea Tow. This time, they pulled us free at about 9 p.m., and we reset the anchor, and surprisingly got a good night's sleep. One thing about anchoring is you must take into account the tidal range. I just keep on learning. In the morning, we checked the prop and everything was OK.

Most boaters seem to have at least one pet, and some have two or three. It's great sport to watch them trying to get their pets to the beach to pee. Sailboaters especially have little dinghies and great big dogs. You must remember that these dogs have been on board without bathroom privileges for sometimes 12 hours. So, in the morning, it is a mass invasion of small craft heading to the one lawn in site where the owner is waiting with a shotgun to discourage these invaders. The dogs jump out of the dinghies and start to pee immediately, usually getting the owner's shorts wet. The dog's masters are being yanked into the water off their dinghies. People are sliding on wet poop. The guy with the shotgun is getting ugly because he sees another wave of dog-laden boats with dinghies on the horizon heading in. Now, usually the dogs take a dip before they get back on their dinghy. Of course, they shake fishy salt water all over their master, who now is just walking with his shoes still on, in a foot of water trying to smile. I can picture his wife saying, "Honey, little 'Itsy Poo' needs a brother to give him some company."

Another thing of beauty is when you visit other people's boats that have cats. That's us too. The big question is where in the hell do you put the litter box. Boats only have so much floor space. A litter box is in reality very large in such small accommodations. They all smell a little.

Jim & Lynda Dunwell - *Patience*

Just to let you know, most people put them on the floor in the head. So here you are, in the middle of the night, trying to take a pee and stubbing your toe on the litter box, causing the litter to fly in all directions.

At Block Island, we saw a first. The boat next to us took their pet to shore for the usual, and I noticed that something seemed a little different on Fido. After another look, we all started to laugh. This couple had a pet pig that had to weigh at least 60 pounds. When we heard the "oink," we couldn't look back. And this is only part of our journey. Be prepared to have a great time and meet wonderful people.

Dismal Swamp Canal, Virginia

Jan & Tracy Nelson - *WANDERIN' STAR*
Punta Gorda, Florida

The simple answer to why we took this trip is: because we like traveling, adventure, and we like boating. Now for the longer answer: whenever we start out on a cruise (short or long), there's kind of a "high" that you get, a smile on your face, and just a happy feeling all over. It's a combination of wanderlust and cruiser lust. Before doing the Great American Loop, we'd been boating and taking cruising trips (usually one to two weeks – our longest being seven weeks in the Caribbean) for about 10 to 15 years.

We decided we wanted to cruise and live full-time on the boat for maybe a period of one to three years. Our current boat is a Hampton 55 Pilothouse powerboat. We have two staterooms and two heads. We picked it up in Norfolk, Virginia, then cruised our boat down to Fort Lauderdale, Florida to outfit it with soft goods (carpeting, upholstery, bedspreads), galley equipment, electronics, dinghy and davit, and so forth. We then cruised down to Key West, Florida, and explored the southwest coast of that state until we reached our Punta Gorda Isles home. On April Fool's Day that same year, after spending two days at the dock of our home, we officially began our trip. We left our home and began what is known as the Great American Loop.

Ever since we were in our twenties, it's been Tracy's dream to retire early. We had recently sold our business, retired, and moved to southwest Florida. When several of our friends and family had serious health issues (including Jan who had a heart operation earlier), and some of them even passed away, we decided that we didn't want to wait much longer to cruise and travel. We have good friends who had recently done the Loop. Tracy first met these two couples through his Rotary Club.

When the wives (Nancy, Bonita, and Jan) became even better friends, we went to a five-day woman's boating course in Sarasota, Florida called Sea Sense; Jan took the course so she'd be more comfortable navigating our boat in ocean conditions, something she didn't have experience with, plus she wanted a boater's overview and knowledge of diesel engines.

Jan wanted to do the Loop from beginning to end. Tracy wasn't so sure. He thought the river part of the Loop from Chicago, Illinois south to Mobile, Alabama, sounded boring, and he really preferred to skip that part. About halfway through (while in Lake Superior), Tracy decided to "humor" Jan and agreed to complete the Loop by doing the rivers system as well.

What did our friends and family think? Comments varied depending on whom you were talking to. We think that most non-boaters thought we were kind of nuts, and were very glad that they weren't going with us. Most asked questions but had no comments. A few said that they'd never want to do what we were doing. Our friends who were boaters had varied thoughts.

Boaters who spent most of their time at the marina asked questions but didn't have comments. We don't think our type of cruising appealed to them. But our boating friends who liked adventure, who liked to get away from the dock and liked to take short cruises; they seemed to be very pleased for us, they emailed us to see what we were doing, and followed our trip via our web page. Several of Jan's girlfriends (non-boaters) joked that they "lived vicariously through Jan" while they watched our web page and we emailed back and forth. One of Jan's sisters, Dianne, thinks, "You're the most courageous person I know." That statement lets you know that she wouldn't consider doing this cruise.

A few more comments from family: Jan's brother, Jere Avenson: "I didn't know that the *Wanderin' Star* would fit in some of the canals in up-state New York, or on the Illinois River. That's ignorance because the big barges travel all those routes. I think that I was most surprised by the path you took through the state of Mississippi ending up in Mobile,

Alabama. Your crossing the Gulf of Mexico at night bothered me a little because of the structural obstructions and slightly submerged floating stuff that you could hit. However, I had a lot of confidence in both of your seamanship skills and I recognized that you both knew what you needed to be aware of. I guess that my concerns were mostly because of my ignorance of the Loop, but I knew that you both were experienced, cautious and capable."

Our son, Stuart Nelson: "I didn't think that you were nuts. Do some people think it is nuts? At the very worst, I would think that some people would think that it is too much work for them, and that they wouldn't want to be gone from home for so long."

We also had friends and family who joined us along the way for brief (usually one-week) periods. We loved having family and friends join us. However, we've learned to leave space (at least a week to two weeks with three weeks being even better) between visiting guests, so we could recoup and relax a little. When you get guests coming almost back-to-back, you get tired and begin to feel like a revolving hotel/restaurant.

It's been an incredible adventure. The places we saw, the people we met, the navigational situations that we worked through and conquered; it was amazing. We didn't realize how poor our geography was.

Obviously, you need to navigate the charts with extreme care and we were traveling at a slow speed, from seven to 17 miles per hour. That speed gives a person a lot of time to observe the geography. We realized that we're visual people, and that we learn the best when we read AND see. Once we have been somewhere and have experienced the sights, the cruising guides seemed to make perfect sense. It was almost as if, when first reading the cruising books about upcoming locations, the pictures were confused and in black and white, but after we had cruised through an area, everything took on vivid colors and then made perfect sense.

One of our very favorite things was taking tours and learning about history along the way. We traveled through the south first, and got a different perspective on things like the War Between the States (what the U.S. history books refer to as the Civil War). After hearing the southerners' comments during tours plus doing a little research, we realized that the U.S. history books didn't give a complete accounting of the war. We found these new historical viewpoints fascinating! When touring a plantation in Charleston, we recognized that the history books didn't do justice to the story of slavery either. Not only did they not give credit to the contributions the slaves brought to this environment, they also didn't explain the complicated structure of the plantations, and how this structure changed over the years. We almost felt as if our history teachers "cheated" us by not spending the time to present the complete story.

As we cruised through the northeastern United States, especially the Hudson River, the routes were full of history of the Revolutionary War. On the Great Lakes, especially when we got into Canadian waters, we heard and read a different variation on the Revolutionary War, and the War of 1812. In the United States history, "We held off the enemy," and in the Canadian perspective, "We contained the enemy." Again, I was intrigued when reading these different points of view. As we cruised through and visited historical sites along the rivers of the Deep South (Kentucky, Tennessee, Mississippi, Alabama), we again heard and read a different accounting of the Civil War. War heroes had different names like Nathan Bedford Forest. We read about how many Union soldiers died, compared to fewer Confederate soldiers. And when we cruised the Bahamas, we again got a different perspective when reading the history of the Loyalists (loyal to England during the American Revolutionary War).

It was interesting to see how much fuel the boat consumed. Rising fuel prices, at the time, made that situation even more interesting! Our boat has electronic fuel gauges that gave us instant fuel consumption readings. At fast speeds (about 17 miles per hour), we get about one-half mile per gallon. At slow speeds (about six to eight miles per hour), we get around three miles to the gallon. I'm not sure we ever would have discovered these details, if not for the locks. The lockmasters call to let each other know how many boats have gone through, and are coming toward the next lock. So, when you leave a lock and head for the next lock, you will usually be waiting for the slowest boat. So why cruise fast? We took it easy, got better fuel economy, and discovered that we really enjoyed that speed. Don't get me wrong though, there are times when we really like the faster speed; like when you're trying to race bad weather, trying to cross the corner of the Gulf of Mexico, crossing the Gulf Stream heading to/from the Bahamas, or scooting across one of the Great Lakes to escape a storm.

One of the very best parts of the cruise was the friendships we made. When we would meet a fellow cruiser, we noticed that we seemed to immediately have so much in common. First of all, we were both the type of people who liked adventure. We immediately had much to talk about. We had similar challenges (navigating, finding fuel at reasonable prices, locating anchorages), problems (mechanical — do you have this part? Have you ever had this problem?), and opportunities (great anchorages, great marinas, great places to tour). If we were lucky enough to be invited aboard, touring other boats was always so much fun. It's amazing how many different boat designs there are!

There were many "best experiences." One of our favorite things to do was take city or area tours, and one of our favorites was in Charleston, South Carolina, which was a city/plantation tour. On the way back from the plantation, the tour guide (a graduate of the Citadel) talked about the Civil War, the Emancipation Proclamation, politics during this time period, slavery, and plantation life... it gave us an entirely new perspective of these subjects, which was fascinating. It made us realize that much of the story was never fully or accurately told when taking history classes in high school and college.

Worst experience would have to be, just in general, when the boat was "acting funny", figuring out what the problem was and getting it fixed. This was a brand new boat for us, so sometimes the "acting funny" was something we hadn't learned about, yet.

We had many favorite areas, so can't narrow it down to just one. Some of these areas included: the Baltimore City Docks and surrounding area, the beautiful Hudson River, the Thousand Island area of the St. Lawrence Seaway, (very scenic), the beautiful Kentucky Lakes area, also scenic, and finally in the Exumas, part of the Bahamas, (the Staniel Cay, Sampson Cay, Fowl Cay area) had great snorkeling. Georgian Bay, Canada, although beautiful, was kind of same-old, same-old for us, since we had cruised here many times before.

In less than one-and-a-half years, we've cruised on this boat over 10,000 statute miles. We locked through a total of 110 times on the trip. After enjoying Christmas with our children in Key West, Florida, we turned northeast and spent almost three months in the Bahamas. We're writing this while we're cruising from the Bahamas (Eleuthera) to Florida (Fort Lauderdale).

Liberty Island - Hudson River, New York

Gerald & Angela Flynn - $\mathcal{U}$NCHAINED
Wildwood, Florida

We are currently on our second Great Loop boat trip. We felt that it was more of an endurance run toward the end of our first trip. So this time, we have decided to really break it down over a three or maybe even a four-year trip. This year, we've decided to just hang out in Michigan and get to know its many lakeside ports. We are also helping very close friends get their boat ready for a trip next year. They want to travel with us down the river system.

We wanted to experience life in slow motion. There is so much to see and do within our own North American boundaries, so we sold our home and moved aboard *Unchained*. We spent several years reading, planning, and taking online boating courses, and we even joined the US Coast Guard Auxiliary to gain a better knowledge of how to travel safely on the water. We have used this knowledge and our many years of experience on more than one occasion, rescuing boats that have gone adrift, and during a rather exciting time of helping a family, whose boat was sinking on the Hudson River. We rescued three children and four adults. We were then assisted by the local and state police rescue boats and helicopter. It makes us feel good to be of service to others.

We are traveling in our 34-foot Thompson Trawler, an aft cabin with a Perkins single engine. *Unchained* has a full/queen walk around bed, a single head, and separate shower. We also have a V-berth with two six-foot bunks with lots of storage. The main cabin also has plenty of storage. There is a single washbasin, but no head in the V-berth. The galley has a cooktop propane stove. I have found that I really don't need an oven. Our inverter handles a slow cooker, and it is great to have a full meal waiting to be enjoyed after a long day's run. We have a full-enclosed flybridge and a lower helm station. We have found that radar makes traveling much easier with changing weather patterns. We also use The Cap'n program, along with our paper charts. *Unchained* offers plenty of comforts, and easily handles two additional crew members.

We are traveling alone this year. We have met wonderful boaters and have done a little buddy boating along the way. We don't get lonely or find a need to be away from each other. Jerry and I get along so well, and the time we are spending with our continued travels has made us at one with our boat. We can sense what each other is thinking or needing at any given moment. We know how to listen to the boat. We do our own maintenance and remodeling together. When we are buddy boating, we have a lot of fun getting to know other boaters with the same interests, and enjoy sharing knowledge and hearing about the crew and their trip experiences.

We don't feel that we have left family and friends behind because many of them have joined us for short visits as we made our way on the Loop. That companionship combined with modern technology (cell phone and wireless Internet) has helped us stay in close contact.

What was the reaction of family and friends to our trip? At first, our children thought we had totally lost our minds, and they kidded, on more than one occasion, about putting us in a home. They couldn't imagine that we were riding bicycles, hiking, and using public transportation to grocery stores to re-provision our boat. After they had a chance to read about our adventures, they became very supportive of our decision to make this trip. Because of our daily journals, many of our friends have purchased either boats or RVs, and started doing their own travel adventures.

We have gained many new and dear friends. We have the feeling of accomplishment and know that what we did is not easily done, but yet, is not an impossible thing to do either.

Our best experience was the entire trip. I cannot define one stop as better than the other. Our worst experience was last summer when we were in the North Channel, Canada, and a sudden storm came up. We had no advanced warning until it was too late. We saw on our GPS that we were 469 yards from the US waters, and we could see the land, and still we spent two hours without moving anywhere. It took all the power we had to just hold position as the waves crashed over our boat. Then, as the storm made its way passed us, we found ourselves caught between both oncoming waves and waves coming from behind. Both would meet and break under our hull. It was a wild ride for a quite a while. We found that *Unchained* could definitely take more of a beating than we could.

As far as what area was our favorite on the trip... wow, that is a hard question to answer because there was so much to see and do. I guess I would say that we first enjoyed meeting a very special group of people who have become our very good friends. We all got to know each other at Waterford, New York. We found ourselves stranded there due to flooding on the Mohawk River.

Because of that, we seized the opportunity to hold a potluck dinner. Eight couples met, talked, shared, and decided to meet and cross wakes for the rest of the trip. Most of the boaters were from Florida, but we dubbed ourselves "The Waterford 8." We have even had a couple of reunions since that first trip. We also found ourselves in a book written by Berkley Duck on MV *Wings*. The name of his book is *Wings on the Great Circle*. Wings was also one of the Waterford 8. We found each section of the trip from Waterford to be challenging, breathtaking, and memorable. We have video of us going down the Big Chute and all you hear is me saying, "My knees are shaking, oh Lord, oh Lord, I can't believe we are doing this." It was exhilarating. From there, it was on to the massive locks on the Mississippi River, and other inland rivers. I just can't put it all into words because I have a huge journal that I tried to condense down, and found it impossible.

All I can say is that each section of the Great Loop tested our wits, wills, love for each other, and instilled a determination in both of us to see it through. Once we finished the trip for the first time, all we could talk about was doing it again, and taking our time. The Great Loop is something that has to be done slowly. There is so much to see that it can be overwhelming to do it as quickly as we did it the first time.

Erie Canal, New York

Laura Tomayko & Ginger Austin -$STARGAZER
Muskegon, Michigan

Why are we called to the sea, to the rivers and to the lakes? Laura and I asked ourselves these and other similar questions. Laura said that she wanted to do something very different from work, home, and day-to-day activities when we retired. Ginger replied that she wanted to be on the water for a long duration, and because it feels "right" as if it's in her DNA.

We purchased our 25-foot Maxum Sun Cruiser and traveled to different ports on Lake Michigan. In Muskegon, we refer to Lake Michigan as the "big lake." This is because we live beside two smaller lakes, which are connected to each other. Our world has often revolved around being on, in, or next to something related to the art or craft of boating in the last 10 years.

When we first heard about the Great Loop, we knew in an instant that doing it would be on our agenda. Laura worried about how we would navigate, and how much our boat could take on a trip such as this. Ginger worried about how we could cook and eat on such a small boat for that long. Our worries proved needless because Ginger had sailed and skippered many powerboats since childhood, and studied many navigational charts the year before we left. Laura fell right into providing the food and plans for it, having learned home economics in college.

We found that on the trip we began to define ourselves differently than in our previous work worlds of school, social work and regulating day care homes and centers. We became captain and first mate. Ginger felt free of the responsibility of meeting the needs of others, emotionally, and Laura began to fantasize how explorers and first Americans ventured forth on the rivers. Our relationship had suffered by working too hard, and thinking too much about work. We both craved the time to be alone with each other. We did find the time to be together, but we were often not alone. We met so many lovely people who were doing what we were doing, and we enjoyed their stories and experiences.

To us, the trip has been life changing. It made us stronger, healthier, and gave us confidence we never had before. We also had to rely on each other's skills and ingenuity, which brought additional respect and interdependence. Each of us developed in ways we had never anticipated. We loved it.

Kirkfield Lift Lock - Trent-Severn Waterway, Ontario

Mary Frye & Rick Gnich - $\mathcal{K}$ISMET
Morley, Michigan

The decision to do the Loop was a partnership decision. We took a number of Power Squadron classes together. We worked on the boat together, making decisions as to improvements needed in equipment and cosmetics. We purchased our 1980 trawler knowing it would take us at least three years to bring it up to our standards.

Our first cruising experience together was in the summer of 1994 when we were dating. We spent six weeks on Rick's Catalina 30 sailboat in the North Channel, Ontario. At that time, Rick had 40 years of boating experience under his belt. I had none... zero, zip, nada! It was quite an adventure. Rick kept telling me we were just a trawler with a stick. It was at that time that he shared his dream of living on a boat. After a couple years of sailing experience under my belt, that dream became a shared goal. We always talk about our current boat finding us. We met the boat when the previous owners were doing the Loop and came into our homeport in Muskegon, Michigan.

Three years later, many hours of research and financial planning, and a little *Kismet* thrown in, we were on our way to Tennessee to pick up our new "home." We then committed the next three summers to bringing this grand old boat back to life. Rick and I are both risk-takers. We like to explore, we don't have to have a plan, and the unknowns that boating presents appealed to both of us. While we loved our home, neither one of us is a pack rat, nor is either one of us attached to "stuff." We are basically unencumbered by family demands. We were fortunate to work with dynamic people in outstanding organizations. With 62 combined years in education, we decided to leave positions that had been extremely rewarding. Career-wise, we both felt we left at the top of our game, a great time to make a move.

We completed our Loop in 10 months, traveling just under 5000 miles. We left our homeport of Arcadia, Michigan, in September and returned to slip number 4 the following July.

We made no advance plans to have travel companions, but did have friends join us for a week on the Tennessee River, which was delightful. We had a number of visitors at different ports, but no other short or long-term, crew. *Kismet* is a 1980 44-foot Gulfstar Trawler, sundeck style. The aft master stateroom has a center queen-size bed, and a head with tub and shower. Forward is a V-berth and second head with shower. Our sundeck is totally enclosed and is our favorite space. Our flybridge is also totally enclosed, which makes for comfortable travel on cool days. We can fit 12 people on the sundeck for happy hour, which makes the boat great for entertaining.

We had a healthy respect for each other's interests, and recognized we would need to have our own time and space while embracing this lifestyle. We made friends easily given the connectedness of the boating community, and found we could be busy all the time if we wanted to. We made good choices as to how we spent our time finding balance between alone and together time.

Family and friends were very supportive, although somewhat skeptical at the permanence of the decision given the fact that we were selling our home. We both had Great Loop maps hanging in our offices, which generated lots of fun conversations with co-workers. Many conversations focused on what we anticipated missing, and how we would accomplish certain tasks. Many in the non-boating community have no understanding of the comforts available on a boat such as ours. One of my secretaries wanted to know where I would get my hair and nails done. Friends from our boating community and from our Power Squadron spoke of living vicariously through our adventure. We realized we were a part of a unique group that wasn't going to just dream... but actually live the dream.

Best experience: We realize this journey was more about relationships than boating. We can talk about the best marina, the best anchorage, best restaurant, but when it comes right down to it, when asked about the best part, we both agree it is the depth of our relationship and the friendships we have made.

Worst experience: Regardless of how prepared you are or how well your boat is equipped, you have experiences that you can't possibly plan for. We were caught in the current at Manasquan Inlet after a fishing boat cut us off at the railroad bridge. With no room to maneuver and the cement bridge within feet of us, *Kismet's* quick-thinking captain wedged the bow between two pilings and secured us. With the assistance of the harbormaster, we put a spring line on the starboard stern side and were able to get back into the channel. We emerged with only minor fiberglass damage.

Our favorite area of the trip was the Trent-Severn Waterway. We have been members of the "Friends of the Trent-Severn" for a number of years, and have dreamed about cruising this area. We had traveled by car to Port Severn several years ago, and looked at the Big Chute and several other locks. The waterway met all of our expectations; rocky shorelines, clear lakes, calm anchorages, winding rivers, good fishing. We approached the lift locks and the Big Chute with some anxiety and much awe. We realize we are a part of a special group of boaters that has had the opportunity to experience this waterway.

Our life philosophy: Happiness is… something to do, something to look forward to, and someone to love. Our Loop experience exemplifies this. We lived this philosophy. There was always something to do – we had defined and shared responsibilities. Rick was the captain, I was the navigator; Rick was the computer geek, I was the communicator; Rick was the mechanic, I was the social director.

We looked forward to every day, and embraced each experience – new waters to cruise, new friends to meet, new marinas, and communities to explore. A friend of mine said you know you really love someone when you can wall paper a bathroom together. I think you really know you love someone when you can live with him or her 24/7 on a boat. Our relationship exceeded the typical friend/companion/lover status to include a safety factor. We relied on and trusted each other to make decisions that kept the boat and us safe. We learned more about each other in our 15 months on the boat than we had in six years of marriage. We laughed at and with each other. Most importantly, our Loop experience taught us to live each day to the fullest.

Trent-Severn Waterway, Ontario

Susan & Michael Fayne - *€*TERNITY
Longboat key, Florida

Eternity is a 1985, 58-foot Hatteras Motor Yacht. Michael and I have been living aboard her in Longboat Key, Florida for 10 years. Here is just a slice of some of the important days on our Great Loop journey...

Journal Entry: Day we left for our trip:
WOW! Here we go again. I'm feeling a mixture of excitement and apprehension as opposed to the beginning of our last journey, when I felt pure excitement. Michael feels the same way. It's because we know a lot more! There WILL be problems; we just don't know when, what, or how serious they'll be – and because of the magnitude of this trip, they could be HUGE. This is how our trip is supposed to go: We start at Longboat Key, then head south through the keys, then north up the Intracoastal Waterway through several sounds, in and out of the Chesapeake Bay and various other bays, and through all kinds of canals, channels and locks. Then we would travel through the Hudson River and Erie Barge Canal, through the Trent-Severn Waterway if the level of water permits, or through four of the Great Lakes, plus others, up and down several rivers including the Mississippi, through the Gulf of Mexico, and then home. So I have reason to be excited and somewhat concerned, especially since my first worry is about going through the very shallow Longboat Pass tomorrow, and Mike's only

worry is about what he'll be having for lunch on the way. With mixed emotions, I'll say goodbye to my home and start this journey with the love of my life, trusting both of us to give our all to this wonderful adventure. How appropriate that this trip is called The Great Loop, our boat being... *Eternity*.

Journal Entry: The best and worst day of our trip was our Anniversary: The Mississippi River...

Happy Anniversary to us! We got up before 6 a.m. As we look out at the Mississippi River from Hoppie's Marina, we feel the promise of a grand day! The fog that's been holding us up is starting to lift. Another boater has offered to help us out so we'll be following him. Our radar has been taken down to accommodate the very low bridges, and our nav lights aren't working properly so we desperately need assistance in the fog. Barring any problems, we should be docked in Paducah, Kentucky, by dark.

Michael's starting to get irritated because the fog isn't lifting as fast as he thought it would, and the other boat has decided that we are slowing them down so they took off, leaving us on our own to contend with the fog. This will cost us more time than we have. Combine that with the fact that we have a long way to go, and a short time to get there. Not a good omen.

OH NO! One of our engines has started to overheat and we had to slow down to a crawl - that doesn't sit well with the captain. This could be a very bad day, and a long one too. This is not fun!

UNBELIEVABLE! At 10a.m.when the engine overheated, Michael knew he needed help. Since we have only been boating for a couple of years, and since Mike isn't mechanical, he needed to talk to the guy that maintains our boat in Longboat Key. (For someone with more experience, this probably wouldn't have been a problem, but for us, it was major.) After a long conversation, it was determined that the trouble in our port engine needed immediate attention, and it couldn't be done while underway.

Michael reluctantly hung up the cell phone with our mechanic's promise he'd wait for him to call back, at which time he would talk Mike through fixing the engine. So, we started looking for somewhere, or something, to tie up to. Our search went on for a long time as we crawled along on one engine. Finally, with the advice of a tow captain, we found a place to pull over, but it was far from the perfect dockage. I wasn't happy about what lay ahead. Chester Prison lies on the bank of the Mississippi River. We couldn't see it from our vantage point, but we did locate their sand barge. Michael tried to hail someone from the prison repeatedly on the radio, and then on the cell phone to see if it was OK for us to stop there, but just our luck - no one answered. It was decided to tie there anyway. We were both petrified!

With Michael yelling instructions to hurry as the current was taking our crippled boat, I got the lines ready and as many fenders as I could find. As the boat approached the miserable barge, my wonderful husband, who is supposed to love me more than life itself, started screaming, "JUMP! JUMP!" I thought, "ME - jump on a sand barge that didn't have great footing - in the middle of the Mississippi River no less - with our boat listing from side to side - is he crazy?"

Nevertheless, we did it - I jumped, got us tied, while Mike struggled against the current with only one engine and no bow thruster to get us docked. What a sight - our beautiful boat covered with dirt and sand, situated against a rocking, disgusting, horrible barge in the middle of the Mississippi River. Making matters worse, we were in front of a prison without permission. I was told to stand watch at the helm in case anyone came. Anyone being a guard? Or perhaps a prisoner? "Isn't this fun?" I thought. In the meantime, Michael, with the cell phone at his ear, toolbox and flashlight in his hand, descended into the engine room to work what would surely be a miracle. I know it was selfish - with him so nervous about performing surgery on the engine, but I was secretly glad to be left alone in the piece and quiet. At the time, the thought occurred to me that making Paducah tonight was probably out of the question. I put that thought on a back burner and decided not to mention it to my already frazzled captain.

I was awakened from my trance with a blood-curdling yell, "SUSAN, HELP!" I knew immediately something horrible had happened. Leaving my post, I ran to the engine room, praying that I wouldn't see blood when I got there. What I did see was my sweet man covered in oil, looking positively defeated. I was so relieved I could have kissed him, if there was only a way to get to him through the mess I was looking at. What had happened? While in the middle of getting instructions from our maintenance guy on how to fix the engine, Michael had dropped the cell phone into the bilge and lost our lifeline. He had tried to get it out using my mop, and in the process created quite a mess. Since my hand was small, I was enlisted to fish it out, take the pitiful looking thing to clean it and get it to work again. As I worked on the dead phone, Michael, without any help, kept working on the engine.

The bad news was that there was oil everywhere, the boat was a mess, we no longer had a cell phone and no one knew where we were. The good news was that the captain fixed the engine, the fog had lifted, and we were on our way south again. We pulled away from the barge without too much trouble considering where we were docked. Where we'll sleep tonight – who knows? Right now – who cares? We were just happy to be away from Chester Prison, that dirty barge, and on our way again.

OH BOY! Where should I start? This day is like a roller coaster; it just seems to go on and on, and up and down. I think it was around 4 p.m. while I was sitting at the helm writing in my journal when Michael announced once again, "I think we've got trouble." It didn't look like we were going to make Paducah after all. So, we set our sights on an anchorage called Angelo Towhead. In the meantime, Michael was trying to reach the boat we had been following out of Hoppie's Marina, but to no avail. We wanted to see if he had made Paducah or was anchored somewhere along the way.

We still weren't very comfortable anchoring in unfamiliar waters alone. When we were almost to the Ohio River, we came across a captain who told us there wasn't enough water at Angelo Towhead to accommodate our boat. He also told us of another place, but he wasn't sure about that one either. Now what? It was now 5 p.m. and dusk was at our doorstep. With no radar and our nav lights not working properly, I was scared, but I knew we'd somehow be OK. The captain, however, didn't feel the same. I wish I could have stayed clear of him, but he needed my help navigating the river. It wasn't easy – Mike, or the river.

We'd been going about five miles, when, out of the blue the boat we had been hailing answered our call. They hadn't made it to Paducah and were tied, illegally, to a barge in the Ohio River. We had been so intent on our course that we had passed them by without noticing. They obviously wanted company on their barge, because the captain was begging us to join them. We weren't very happy with him for deserting us in the fog, but decided we didn't have much of a choice. So we turned around and started heading toward them when, out of nowhere, appeared another captain on a boat we had docked next to in Chicago. When he saw us going the opposite direction, he immediately called us. It wasn't difficult for him to convince us to forget the other boat with their barge, and follow him instead. He was going to Paducah and he assured us he would go slowly so we could take advantage of his radar, lights, and expertise. So, we turned around one more time. Mike called the other boat to give them the bad news. When they heard we weren't going to tie up with them, they decided to leave what I'm sure was a bad spot, and join us. Soon, we had a convoy of three going down the Ohio River in the dark. Everything was great for a short time. Mike was relaxing. We were the middle boat, and our friends were watching over us. However, the weather was picking up now, which meant we needed to make new plans. We had many questions, but we let our friend, who was a real captain, make the decisions for us. We'll go through Lock 52 and tie up on a barge after the lock. It was pitch black now and very hard to see. We soon realized that the captain didn't know where he was going either. It turned out the lock he was looking for was under construction, and not open so we passed it by and went on to the lock which was operating right then. The lockmaster was a gem. After locking us through, he realized the danger we could be in if we continued down the river at night in the bad weather, and although he wasn't supposed to, he offered us a spot behind his lock to dock our boats for the night. It was a miserable location, but who cared?

It was late, but it was still our anniversary and we were all hungry. We needed a drink or two, or maybe 10, so we invited everyone over for a party. We had a good time with our friends. This was truly an unforgettable anniversary.

Journal Entry: Last day on the water:
The Gulf of Mexico…

How can one be happy and sad at the same time? It's a strange feeling. I can't wait to get home, but I don't want this wonderful journey to end. Mike is also having mixed emotions. It's late morning and we're still in bed, lost in our own thoughts and recalling, to one another, some of the great times, and some of the not-so-great times we've had over the past several months.

At 10 AM, we started our cruise to Longboat Key, Florida. The gulf was choppy; the skies were my favorite shade of blue, and very clear. When we saw Anna Maria Island, the chills started. I couldn't get enough pictures of this part of our trip - it all felt so significant. By the time we spotted Longboat Key, we were both visibly emotional - cheering, laughing, crying, hugging, and kissing - it went on and on. At channel marker #15 the emotions started all over again. We couldn't stand that it was ending, and we couldn't believe we had made it all this way. We didn't want our adventure to be over, but we were so very happy to be coming home. There was a myriad of emotions. What a spectacular moment when we pulled into our slip! Our friends were there to greet us. Any traces of sadness were replaced by excitement and pure joy.

WE DID IT! This very adventurous couple with very little experience at this task had accomplished more than anyone could ever have known. With little planning, we had embarked on a journey that would surely test us in many ways. We had worked together endlessly, relying on one another's strengths as we met the many challenges we faced. The wonderful friends we made and the fascinating places we traveled were a major part of this wonderful time in our lives. How special that we have gained a new closeness because of it.

What I'll remember most is Michael and I sharing this romantic adventure, for everything I know of love and everything I love of life revolves around the two of us. We spent so much intense time together fulfilling this exciting dream that tonight we feel like celebrating - just the two of us who have shared so very much already.

Trent-Severn Waterway, Ontario

Nette Feller - *Ooh Ga Cha Ka*
Oostburg, Wisconsin

When I was young, my parents took me to visit Mobile, Alabama, where they had spent much of their earlier married life. During the trip, we spent a great deal of time around the Mobile area, where we met several people who were heading out onto the Gulf. Two years later, we were in Washington DC, again near the water, and visited with travelers there as well.

While living on Lake Michigan in my youth, these visits just sparked a life-long interest in traveling on the water.

I later found out that the first person in my maternal grandmother's family to come to America was an Irish Sea captain, who sailed his family over on his own ship. Must have been one heck of a trip! No one in the family since has been involved with water travel until me.

I did the trip with my now former spouse in a 1972 30-foot Calkins Bartender that we refurbished. Our route was Lake Michigan; Cal-Sag, Illinois, Mississippi, Ohio and Cumberland Rivers; Kentucky Lake, Tennessee River (all the way to Knoxville and back), Tennessee-Tombigbee Waterway, Caloosahatchee River, Intracoastal Waterway, Dismal Swamp, and Hudson River. Then on to Erie Canal to Oswego, Lake Ontario; Trent-Severn Waterway, Georgian Bay, North Channel, Canada; Les Cheneaux Islands, Lake Michigan, Beaver Island,

Washington Island, and on down to Racine, Wisconsin, for a total of 6,713 miles and 122 locks.

What were the practical aspects of the boat? She had a lot of storage so I carried about six months worth of dry/canned goods on board. The best part was being surrounded by water and the just "ease on by" attitude we adopted from the push boat captains.

Boating friends we left behind were especially fond of us since we called them during the winter and shouted, "We're on the boat - you're not!" Some family tracked us on charts that we left with them. Most said, "A 30-foot boat? You are nuts."

I gained a feeling of accomplishment from doing something that not many people would, or even would want to do. It was also a challenge doing the Loop on a 30-foot boat that didn't have many amenities (but I crammed in as many as I could). Mostly I gained the knowledge that it was a lifestyle that I enjoyed, and I look forward to doing it again.

The first time we did the trip, each day was always started with a: "Thank you Lord for this day - don't let us hit a push boat!" And a bit of anxiety not knowing where to revisit.

Best rush? Singing Eternal Father at Annapolis Naval Chapel, with the knowledge that we had arrived by boat. Worst experience? Anchoring almost on shore on the Ohio River in a very strong current, as a group of boats couldn't go through the lock that night. We spent the night watching everyone's lights dance around, trying to make sure we had kept our anchorage position.

Best place? Hoppie's - where we met some of our best boat buddies who we traveled with on and off throughout the whole trip.

Worst place? Racine, Wisconsin - but only because it meant the end of the trip!

The Big Chute - Trent-Severn Waterway, Ontario

John & Judy Gill - *Two J's U*
Hatboro, Pennsylvania

We did the Great Loop Cruise over three boating seasons. We took this amount of time so that we could go slower than most seemed to go, we wanted to see and do everything we had planned, without being rushed with time restraints of any kind. We also wanted to go slow and smell the roses.

We broke our Loop into three boating seasons because Judy's mother is in a nursing home, and we wanted the flexibility of being able to go home if necessary. We did not want to be away from our home and friends for a whole year or more at one time, and we wanted to spread the costs over three years.

Our boat is a gasoline powered 36-foot Carver Mariner, which has a raised bridge. She has a master stateroom, a bunk bed guest cabin, a full head with a separate shower, galley, and a large saloon and aft deck seating area. The raised bridge has a full, wide, walk around, which makes locking much easier than most boats. We have 96 gallons of house water, a 30-gallon holding tank for black water waste, and 337 gallons of fuel. The galley has a three-burner stove, full refrigerator with freezer, a microwave oven and a broiler/oven.

The America's Great Loop Cruise had been a dream of ours for more than 20 years. Judy's family had vacationed on Sparrow Lake on the Trent-

Severn Waterway for more than 60 years. John's parents owned a cottage on the northern tip of Moon Island (Fry Point) at Sans Souci, Ontario, in the Georgian Bay. While vacationing on Sparrow Lake, we watched as many American boats pass by the Lodge at the north end of the lake, and learned about this circumnavigation of the eastern half of the United States and Canada. We both have been boaters since early childhood, and purchased our cruiser for the express purpose of doing the Loop. As part of our homework and preparations, we joined the America's Great Loop Cruisers' Association (AGLCA) as Charter Members.

We also attended a West Marine's Trawlers Fest in Solomon, Maryland, on the Chesapeake Bay, where we attended several seminars, one by Ron and Eva Stob, the founders of AGLCA.

We spent about four years getting ready for the cruising adventure of a lifetime, starting with early retirements each. We outfitted the boat for long range cruising and living aboard for long periods of time. Before we started the Loop, we had not been on our boat for more than 11 days at a time, but had been on our friend's boat for 26 days, helping them take their boat from the Chesapeake Bay to Florida on the ICW.

Another couple did the Loop with us aboard their own boat. We are close friends with them and have cruised together several times in the past. It was great sharing the navigation chores, and we had community dinners most nights. We only had guests on board for three weeks the first year, and two weeks the second year. All guests were boat knowledgeable, and had passed a safe boating education course (our requirement for long range cruising with us).

We did the route in three boating seasons. The first summer, we left the Chesapeake Bay and did the Lake Champlain route, Montreal, Ottawa, Rideau Waterway, 1000 Islands, Trent-Severn Waterway, Georgian Bay to Parry Sound and then to Tobermory, down the Ontario side of Lake Huron and into Lake Erie. We wintered over in LaSalle, Michigan the first winter – 1,935 miles.

The second summer we cruised Lake Erie to Put-in-Bay, Ohio and then up the Michigan side of Lake Huron to Lake Superior (a brief one-day visit to be able to say we have had our boat in all five great lakes). We then went down the east side of Lake Michigan (the Michigan side) to Chicago, Illinois, then down the heartland rivers to Mobile, Alabama.

We took a side trip, by boat, up the Cumberland River to see the Grand Ole Opry, in Nashville, Tennessee. From Mobile, Alabama, we did the rim route down Florida's West Coast to Fort Myers and then across the Okeechobee Waterway to Stuart, Florida, and north to Fort Pierce, Florida, where we wintered over the second winter – 3,357 miles.

The third summer we cruised up the East Coast ICW from Fort Pierce, Florida, to the Sassafras Harbor Marina in Georgetown, Maryland on the Chesapeake Bay – 1,432 miles.

Our friends and family were happy that we were able to make our dream come true, and were very supportive. We kept in touch with family and friends by writing daily logs and e-mailing them in groups of four to five, when we had written a page or two. We were amazed how many people we sent e-mails to that were forwarding our logs to others (almost double our circulation). Many actually kept track of our whereabouts and progress on a map. We also kept in touch via cell phone with many of our relatives and friends, including the couple taking care of our home.

The reaction of most upon our completion is one of awe, particularly those in our marina, and the marina owner who now looks up to us and introduces us to people as the couple who completed the Loop. Conversely, there are some who showed little or no interest and did not attend any of our two 35mm scripted slide presentations - because the Loop is not something that they will ever be able to do. We think that many people simply do not like to learn about things that they will not be able to do someday.

How did we survive the close quarters? When we bought our boat, one of the criteria was having a door to slam (not just a privacy curtain). The first year, it was slammed once, the second year, shut gently twice, and the third year not at all! Living in close quarters, we learned that most people just needed a bit of time to themselves, which must be respected. For us, it was a marriage strengthening experience, and we learned to work together, a lesson, we believe, that will carry over into our retired life. At one time, Judy even forgot she was on a boat!

The best experience is all the wonderful people we met, and the lifelong friends we made while cruising on the Loop, and by attending an AGLCA Rendezvous.

We only had one bad experience, when a boater threatened our boat twice because he thought an American should not have an electric outlet spot at one of the lock docks on the Rideau Waterway. He had also had too much to drink, and we had to call the Ontario Provincial Police. It was the only time we have ever locked our boat from a cleat to the dock with a steel cable!

Our favorite was definitely the Rideau Waterway; starting with the Ladder Locks (an eight-step lock at Ottawa), being in Ottawa over the Dominion Day weekend and then down this beautiful and untarnished waterway to the 1000 Islands on Lake Ontario. Next was the Trent-Severn Waterway from Lake Ontario to the Georgian Bay. It was a thrill to take our cruiser into areas that we have boated in a runabout for many years, particularly the Marine Railway at Big Chute on the northern Trent-Severn Waterway. Our 17-foot Bowrider was the first boat of its size to go over the new railway when built in 1977.

We wanted to see the countries, both the United States and Canada, by water versus the highways and interstate roads. One objective, not realized, was to see if there was a place where we could live in the future that would be on or near the water, instead of our Philadelphia suburb. We currently have a two-hour drive to our boat, which we keep docked on the Chesapeake Bay.

What we gained is the fulfillment of a lifelong dream, and not having to say someday when we got older, "Why didn't we do that?" So many of our friends have told us to simply do the things you really want to do, and so that you will not regret not having done them later in life. We have also learned how to slow down, smell the roses, and take it one day at a time.

Fox Island - North Channel, Ontario

Janet & Bob Halderman - *Heaven Too*
Charlevoix, Michigan

My wife and I are taking this trip by ourselves, along with another couple, good friends of ours who will be traveling with us, but on their own boat.

Our boat is a 46-foot Cruisers Yacht 455. It is a crossover between an express and an aft-cabin model. We have a forward guest cabin and head, a side cabin, and the master cabin in the stern with its own head. The boat is 15-and-a-half feet wide and is livable for long periods. We are comfortable cruising at 10 miles per hour or at 28 miles per hour. We have enough holding tank capacity to go for three weeks without dumping, as long as we don't have guests. We have satellite TV, and an excellent galley. With all the boats we've owned, this boat is by far the best for doing the Great Loop.

As we do this trip, I turn 70, my wife turns 68, and we were looking for new challenges, new adventures, something to keep our minds working and to keep us young. I had read about the Great Loop several years ago, and always thought that it might be something we should do. However, I never owned a boat that I wanted to live on for several months at a time. Our boats have been primarily express models where you live "down in" on bench seats in cramped quarters. My youngest son said it would be fun to have a boat to cruise in "up north" that would comfortably handle his family of wife and two kids, plus my wife and me. That got me to looking at boats and the Cruisers Yacht 4450 came to mind. The 4450 had three cabins, a bridge like our expresses, and it should fill the bill. Then I learned about the updated version of the 4450, which is the 455. The 455 is 18 inches wider in the cabin and that made a world of improvement, and it met our goals perfectly.

We already have had one friend and a couple travel with us. The one friend, a widower, traveled with us for 10 days, and the couple traveled with us for four days. We prefer to travel without guests, but will probably have a few more couples join us at various stages of the trip. The only family members to join us will be our one son, his wife and two children, who will join us for the first week of April when their daughter is on spring break. Our thoughts on guests are that it is much easier to travel without them. With guests, you feel like you have to entertain them all the time, and few guests know how to help, or even want to help with the daily chores of a boat. We have had several couples travel with us for a week over the years, and only one couple ever meshed right in with the boating duties and activities. All other couples tended to watch, and wait to be waited upon.

Life aboard is much more relaxing when we are traveling alone, the two of us, with our dog. Our good friends traveling on their own boat along with us create no problems at all. They have their own boat, we have ours, we get together on one boat or the other two or three times a day, and otherwise they do their thing and we do ours. We plan where we are going and what we'll do, and since we have boated together for so many years, our ideas mesh well.

As we analyzed the trip, we felt the obvious way to do it was to start in late summer from the Great Lakes, work our way to the Tennessee River, and wait for hurricane season to end, then head for the Gulf. Tour Florida in the winter, maybe go to the Bahamas, and then head north in the spring. Then go to the Erie and Oswego Canals, do the Thousand Islands, then do the Trent-Severn Waterway and be back in the Great Lakes by July.

We didn't leave as early as we had planned due to business opportunities, a family business my sons now run, so we left the Thursday after Labor Day. Our plans were to be back at our summer home on Lake Charlevoix sometime in July. However, we were flexible since plans have a way of changing on this type of trip.

I'm not one to own a cottage on one lake, or a trailerable boat to boat on one reservoir. I like to go to new waters, I like to explore, and

Janet & Bob Halderman - *Heaven Too*

I like to see new sights. Fortunately, my wife does too.

So, with a great boat, being retired, and having the money to take the trip, we decided to do the Loop. Our family encouraged us to do so, and we were sure it would provide us with the challenge and adventure we were seeking. I researched the trip, joined AGLCA, purchased all the newsletters, and researched the Great Loop on the web. All the information I obtained said, "Go do it."

Then, during the summer a big hurricane hit, fuel became high-priced and scarce, and we reconsidered our decision. We had some people say, "Don't go," and others that said by the time we got going, fuel wouldn't be a problem and the major hurricane damage was not in our path. At the age of 70, we decided if we were going, we needed to just go, since we doubted if fuel prices would ever be any better. As conditions have proved out, going was the right decision.

All our friends thought the trip sounded like a wonderful adventure, and were envious of our being able to actually do it. Our family thought it was a great idea, and they encouraged us to make the leap.

We hoped to see country we've never seen before, and wouldn't see unless we were on a boat. We hoped to make many new friends, and we knew this trip would be a wonderful new learning experience. The trip has been all we hoped for. The river cruising got to be a little long, and since arriving on the Gulf Coast, the trip has been much more enjoyable. We've met many nice people, both boaters on the Loop and people we've just met along the way. The most outstanding feature is the friendliness of the people we've met. The trip has been relaxing but also an adventure. You never know when you're going, when you'll get there, or what you'll do along the way. Plans continuously change. You can't make reservations much further than a few hours ahead. You rapidly learn to go with the flow, don't fight it, lay back and enjoy it. And enjoy it, we have.

The best answer to the question on what type and size boat you should have for this trip has been, "The smallest you can be comfortable in, and the most you can afford." That is good, but I would add if you are going to spend most of a year or more living on board, try to get a boat with the most creature comforts and similarity to home that you can afford. We cruised many years with a 23-foot Slickcraft and we would set up a kitchen on shore. We could do the Loop in a 23-foot boat but it wouldn't be enjoyable for us. Our friends who are boating with us don't have satellite TV. They have found that not having it makes their trip much less enjoyable. When you're used to getting the news, the weather, and watching "24" on Monday night, you feel you're paying a price that you don't enjoy paying. Of course, they are welcome to come over on our boat to watch all those things, and I believe during Christmas break, the wife may get the husband talked into a satellite TV.

We left Charlevoix early September, and went home for Thanksgiving for one week, and came home for Christmas for three weeks. The breaks in the action, especially when you have a family business and five grandchildren all within five miles of where we live in Indiana, have all been very enjoyable.

North Channel, Ontario

Mike & Paige Caldwell - GOLDEN
Cape Coral, Florida

Both my husband and I grew up on boats, boating seemed to fill our lives. We've lived aboard for five to six months every year since 2002, and previous to that, we were on board every weekend, no exceptions; vacations were sailing trips in the Caribbean. But for me, this trip is a consolation prize: this is second to what my dream had always been, but since I can't do that, we chose to do what we can. Let me explain...

When I was a child, my parents took my two siblings and I out of school and on my father's 36-foot sailboat; we sailed from Burlington, Vermont to Grenada (southern Caribbean) then back to Florida, hitting every island along the way. I raced sailboats all through high school and college, sailed from Virginia to the US Virgins, and sailed extensively in the Caribbean (in their later years, my parents were nice enough to move there with their 43-foot sailboat). Sailing to foreign destinations is what my family did. From the moment that first long sailing trip of my youth ended, I wanted to sail around the world. No question about it.

In 1984, while in college, I was in a car accident that left me with a fused spine. For the first 10 years after that fusion, I could pretty much do as I pleased as my back was in decent shape. I married my husband, sold him on sailing, and started working on the idea of sailing around the world. He was game, sold his powerboat, and we bought a sailboat, a Catalina 34. It was a great lake boat and a good boat on which to teach

Mike how to sail. We raced every week as crew on a friend's boat, and Mike got really good at sailing.

About 10 years after my spinal fusion, the vertebrae around the fusion started to deteriorate, and it was only a few years after that before I realized that I could no longer sail on the lake, much less contemplate doing long-distance ocean sailing. That was a really bad day, the day I realized that my big dream was out of reach. Sailing around the world had been my one big dream, and one that could have otherwise been realized with my willing spouse and stable finances.

With that dream in ashes, we looked around and said, "OK, we love boats, what can we do that my back can handle?" The first thing we did was sell the sailboat and buy *Golden*, our trawler. We've had her for eight years now. Rough days on the water can still wear me out, but for the most part, it's a much less physical lifestyle than sailing. Looking for challenges we could tackle on the trawler, we started reading and realized that there were huge opportunities in the lakes, rivers and canals within the United States and Canada – so we started taking trips: the Erie to visit my alma mater Cornell on Cayuga, New York; the Rideau Canal loop and the St. Lawrence out to the Saguenay, Quebec. We found that we loved it. It wasn't what I had originally thought I'd be doing, but it was still wonderful. So, yes, while this is a consolation prize, and not my original dream, we love the inland waterways.

As far as leaving home and friends, I had always anticipated sailing and traveling in places where I didn't speak the language, and couldn't get food that I recognized, or replacement parts for the boat that I needed. This trip is all in the US and Canada – we're NOT leaving the comforts of home! We have access to all the same goods and services we have at our house, and anything we might desire or need is just an overnight package away. Quite frankly, it's easy cruising! We've got satellite TV, Wi-Fi, Internet, cell phones – heck, we're never out of touch. So much so that I sometimes threaten to turn everything off so that I can feel like I am away from home.

The other thing that should be said – even though it's probably obvious by now - is that unlike many couples, this boat is not my husband's, and I, being the wife, am not just going along on his adventure. This is very much a shared passion, and the running of the boat is a shared job. I can drive the boat almost as well as him; but if it's really windy, I'd just as soon he drive it, since if we hit something, I'd rather he did it since he'll just give me grief to no end. When he hits something, that's just bad luck and that's the end of it! Anyway, my point is that this is truly a shared adventure.

Our friends are envious! Everyone we've talked to about doing the Loop has been jealous and supportive. As I mentioned earlier, my family has a history of traveling, so this comes as no surprise to them.

We hope to gain better knowledge of our country and its history, and acquire an intimate acquaintance with its geography. We also hope to gain more friends, and more boating experience – you can never have too many!

As for living on the boat vs. living on land – the trawler is big enough that we're not even close to being cramped. Our boat is a 1988 38-foot Tradewinds Trawler, made by Marine Trader. She's an aft cabin model so she has a spacious master with a centerline queen bed, private head with shower, and lots of built in storage. We've got guest accommodations forward consisting of bunk beds, a double on top, single on the bottom. Also forward is a second head. The galley is down; the main saloon has barstools for two, with a long settee and a comfy chair. The back deck is wonderful, large, spacious, and outfitted with white wicker, two chairs and a love seat. The flybridge has two helm seats and seating for five to six people. The whole flybridge and aft deck are enclosed in canvas/isinglass, making her very comfortable in all weather. She's an incredibly comfortable live aboard cruiser. We travel at 8-9 knots at an economical 5.4 gallons per hour (twin Cummins diesels), and our top speed is 12 knots if we feel like burning huge amounts of fuel - which we never, ever do.

When we moved from Vermont to Florida a few years ago, we sold off most of our northern furniture, opting to buy new stuff in Florida. For the last month that we lived in our Vermont home, we had the following furniture (everything else had been sold): our bed, two barstools, and one couch. We realized after a few weeks that we weren't using the house any differently than we'd ever used it! Though the house had been filled with tons of furniture and stuff, yet all we really used was our bed (sleeping), the two bar stools at the kitchen counter (eating) and the couch (reading and TV). All that other stuff apparently was just for show, and we didn't even know it! Had you asked us before we sold it all off, I'm sure I would have replied, "I need all this stuff." Ha! What did I know!

We moved onto the boat for a year just after that, and guess what - on board I have a bed, two barstools and a couch. We're all set. Living on the boat is a breeze - especially after the sailboat that was comparatively much smaller. I don't even think about it as being different from home. I've heard about people who pull into port every once in a while only to get a hotel room so they can be on land for a night or two, and I've never understood it. I'd rather be on the boat than be at home!

As for living in such close quarters, I have to admit that I don't think about it much since we've done it for so long. Having spent a few days trying to come up with something, I'd have to say compromise and learning to bite my tongue go a long way toward a happy relationship. Not that I'm always able to do so, and it may be harder for me than the typical boating wife, because I know almost as much about boats/boating/navigation/systems as my husband. On board, we're equals with two strong opinions, and that makes for some strong differences in opinion at times.

Fortunately, we've been married 16 years and are fairly alike. Most of our arguments come from operating the boat - I'm ultra-conservative, and I know I drive him nuts with some of my conservative tendencies. The problems arise because I'm the navigator; I choose and plot courses that are more conservative than he would choose to do (deeper water, further from buoys, slightly longer courses, etc.). I've learned to give in where I can; he's learned to bend to accommodate me. Still, tempers flare now and then. Living in a fairly small space, we both try to get over our funk and move on – small living quarters force intimacy, and that's no fun when you're annoyed at one another. Again, I'm not great at this yet, but I've learned that it makes life a lot better when I can make it happen.

Our worst experience while on the trip was when we were taking the boat down the Jersey shore on the way to Florida. The forecast turned out to be wrong, and we were a few miles off shore, rolling like mad in beam seas. Rolling so much that our props were coming out of the water – a pretty good feat for props three to four feet below the water! A few miles from the Manasquan Inlet, our bilge alarm came on – and didn't shut off. Mike went down below to check the bilges, and found water up to the base of the engine mounts. He raced up to let us know what he'd found, we pulled out life jackets and were making plans on what to do if we couldn't get ahead of the water coming in. Fortunately, within another 60 seconds, Mike came back up and announced that the water in the bilge wasn't seawater, but that our fresh water tank hose had let go, and emptied all 200 gallons into the bilge.

Mike & Paige Caldwell - *Golden*

Those few minutes from the time the bilge alarm went off to the time Mike found the cause were the longest and scariest of my boating career. I had visions of the boat sinking out from underneath us a few miles from the Jersey shoreline.

Best experience: Playing in the rapids at Bad River in the Georgian Bay. We had a great time running up and down the rapids in our dinghy, and we made fast friends with another couple on a trawler, who happened to dinghy by and were looking for the scoop on what rapids to run. We had great fun, saw incredible scenery, and met some great people. We met up with those folks several times over the next few weeks as we worked our way through the North Channel, and we remember them fondly.

I seriously doubt that we'll enjoy anything more than we enjoyed the northern Georgian Bay and the North Channel in Canada. We love places that are challenging, out of the way, difficult to navigate and gorgeous in their scenery. The northern portion of the Georgian Bay and the North Channel is our idea of paradise, and we had them mostly to ourselves. World politics and fuel prices are keeping people home – places that the guidebook said would be crowded simply weren't. We could enjoy the splendors of the Georgian Bay and the North Channel in solitude.

Mackinaw Island, Michigan

Ted & Helen Brown - c*A*CT II
Madison, Wisconsin

We often feel a little guilty, maybe irresponsible, when we talk with people who have planned for years and years to do significant cruising trips after they retire. We responded to the "call of the water" in a very impromptu, spontaneous way. Helen was driving home from a workout at the YMCA in Madison, Wisconsin, when she spotted a 25-foot Sea Ray Sundancer sitting in a commercial parking lot, listed for sale. After a closer look and jotting down the contact number, she came back home and casually said to Ted, "You remember last Sunday, after spending another day of looking for a larger house, and I suggested that we use our money for doing other things?" Well, I hadn't finished that sentence... "I think we should buy a boat." Ted's response with 60 years of minimal boating experience was simply "OK." We often kid that it frequently takes him much longer to respond to the question, "What would you like for dinner tonight?"

Anyway, that preliminary, rather impulsive, almost idle conversation started us off on an adventure we could never ever have dreamed of having. We bought a 25-foot Sundancer with the cuddy cabin. We named her, fittingly enough, Mood Struck, and we started experimenting and trying things out. Our first summer took us to the Mississippi River and a trip from Trempleau, Wisconsin, to St. Paul, Minnesota, about 250 miles, while sleeping six nights on the boat.

Helen grew up near the river and was fortunate enough to have had a cottage for a period of time at Dakota, Minnesota. This gave her ample viewing of the barges and leisure boats traveling south down the river. From this experience in her youth, an almost seemingly impossible dream was formed... to take a boat all the way down the Mississippi to the Gulf of Mexico. Early on, we learned that this wasn't the most desirable option, and taking the Ohio River, Tennessee River, and the Tennessee-Tombigbee Waterway is a much more boat-friendly route.

Plans were soon underway to head out the following summer, in late August, to see how far we could get. The theory was, when it's not fun any longer, we'll go home and get the truck and trailer and end the adventure. Well, we started out in Prairie du Chien, Wisconsin, often being the only pleasure boater out on the waters, and even more so after we passed Dubuque, Iowa, on Labor Day weekend. Once we got to Hoppie's Marina, just south of St. Louis, a new kind of excitement (education) began, and we were wide-eyed much of the time. We had become part of a caravan. We didn't know about all of the people who traveled south for the winter, by boat. We had never heard of doing the "Great Loop." In addition, as we were most always in the smallest boat at the dock, we had no idea of the wonderful accommodations that were accessible for "regular folks." We were in awe, and we were jealous. We wanted to be able to do this too.

We continued traveling in our little boat, with its close quarters, for a total of three-and-a-half months, until we reached Pensacola, Florida. It also included a side trip to Chattanooga, Tennessee. Then we had to make a decision whether or not to paint the bottom of the boat in order to stay in salt water (another totally foreign idea to us). It was getting cool, which meant that we had to stay inside for much more time each day; the lack of daylight savings time did an unexpected number on us as well. So, we headed back to cold Wisconsin with our minds boggling with ideas.

Within the next two years, Ted had a triple by-pass, read Chapman's cover-to-cover, and followed the travels of *Ladybug*, a catamaran circumnavigating the world. We attended several Trawler Fests; there were endless hours logged on yachtworld.com. We sold our house in 40 minutes during the first open house, and our vehicles were gone shortly thereafter. Suddenly, we were homeless and boat-less. A used motor home was the first purchase we made, and we started traveling wherever we thought there might be a suitable boat. It was a long (nine months) endeavor with several frustrating surveys on potential boats before we made the purchase: an Albin 43-foot Sundeck trawler that would now be our "home." We named her *Act II*, representing our two loves... our two passions - boating and theatre, and we had the comedy/tragedy faces painted on her stern – and oh, how prophetic those two faces would become.

Act II would take us up or down the East Coast four times, around the northern route through all of the Great Lakes, and another trip around the top across Lake Ontario into the Thousand Islands. Cruising the Trent-Severn Waterway, Georgian Bay, North Channel and the Sault Ste. Marie locks brought us close to closing the Loop for the second time.

The highlights were many. To name a few of our favorites: docking at the theatre in Gananoque, Ontario, so we could go in to see their show, cruising overnight across Lake Michigan into the Green Bay, meeting fascinating people who always added new information to our list of places we now wanted to go, tying to a mooring ball in the Hudson River so we could take the subway to a theatrical production, and come back "home" to sleep in our own bed.

However, the dirt has beckoned. After 17,000 miles of cruising, we purchased a land base near Appleton, Wisconsin, thus allowing another lucky couple to take *Act II* for the joyride of their lives. We'll keep boating, it's in the blood, just how, where, and when, we're not sure, but we have an ongoing list that we feel certain will outlive us.

Mackinaw Island, Michigan

Scott & Cyndi Perkins - *Chip Ahoy*
Houghton, Michigan

We have completed two Great Loops aboard our 32-foot Downeast sailboat *Chip Ahoy*. We began both in Houghton-Hancock on the west end of Lake Superior. The first Loop took approximately nine months, the second circumnavigation lasted 10 months. A great deal of motoring was required, along with mast unstepping when entering the river system, and again on the upbound upon entering the Erie Canal. Under sail or engine power, we usually move at five to seven miles per hour, with the exception of the Mississippi River, where the zippy current gave us a big boost in speed. On the Ohio River, opposing current on our full keel knocked us down to the three-to-five miles per hour range. Since the journey is the major point of the whole experience, we weren't overly concerned with how fast we were going, although a common non-boater question is, "How long did it take you?"

Our boat is very seaworthy, but even more important to this trip is that Scott is a technician and a handyman who is very adept at fixing things on the fly with a MacGyver-like talent when called for. We are happy to have completed two Loops slowly and safely, with enough emergency adrenaline rushes under our belts to know that surprises will happen, and that we can rise to nearly every occasion. Many people have helped us out during these times, and we are sure there are angels sitting on our shoulders. In turn, we have acquired a self-reliance that allows us to continue confidently, exploring new territory, aboard *Chip Ahoy.*

We traveled mostly as a couple, as we have during more than a decade of sailing on Lake Superior. Back then our teenagers were mad at us for giving up the RV and runabout camping/boating lifestyle. They didn't take to sailing. After 25 years of marriage and raising a family, the time alone cruising as a couple has been thoroughly savored. We do enjoy infrequent visitors. On the second Loop our 23-year-old son Scotty joined us at Solomon's Island, Maryland, for the remainder of the trip up the Chesapeake, down the Delaware, into New York Harbor, and up the Hudson River into the canal systems. It was a pleasant novelty to have a third hand in the locks; my husband and I were used to fending for ourselves, and surprised at how much fun it was to have additional help and companionship. We appreciated the opportunity to share our cruising lifestyle with our son. It seems to us that most family and friends just don't "get" what it's like to make this journey. Scotty got an up close and personal taste of the adrenaline rushes, the drudgery and the spectacular moments of wonder that would unexpectedly unfold during all the phases of cruising.

Chip Ahoy is a heavy blue water cruising vessel with a modified full keel. Built for ocean crossings, she is capable of handling anything that comes her way. A solar panel and wind generator ensure our self-sufficiency. Anchored out in the Keys for nearly two months, we only had to run the engine briefly on two occasions (cloudy and still days) in order to charge up the batteries. We lost our refrigerator just before our second Loop. So, from Lake Superior to Mobile Bay, we used our big icebox in the galley. We now know that, like pay phones, block ice is on its way to extinction in America. We invested in a new refrigerator/freezer unit just in time for Thanksgiving. Scott, the electronics whiz, installed it at Eastern Shores Marina in Fairhope, and we hosted another boater for an oven-baked turkey dinner with all the trimmings at the Ingram Bayou anchorage.

Our first trip was roughly 6,000 miles. We traveled Lake Superior's Keweenaw Peninsula down Lake Michigan into the Heartland Rivers, the West Coast of Florida, East Coast of Florida, up the U.S. eastern seaboard, into New York Harbor, up the Hudson River, and through the entire Erie Canal to Lake Erie. From there, we traveled up the Detroit River, through Lake St. Clair, the St. Clair River, and into Lake Huron. From Lake Huron, we entered St. Mary's River, which leads to the Sault Ste. Marie Lock, and our breathtaking Lake Superior. On the second

Loop, we explored alternate routes, anchored out more as opposed to staying in marinas, and lopped off 400 miles or so by hopping off the Erie Canal, taking the Oswego Canal to Lake Ontario, and ultimately the Trent-Severn Waterway. By the time we completed the Trent-Severn, we were tired of rock shoals, tight spaces, and skinny water, and so we struck out across Georgian Bay into Lake Huron in a wide-water homeward-bound marathon, stopping only briefly to fuel up in Detour, Michigan, and spending just one night in Marquette before the final 10 hours home to Houghton-Hancock.

Our standard joke is that we Looped for a second time because we are gluttons for punishment. Actually, we'd hoped to take the eastern seaboard south for the winter the second time. The extreme hurricane season prompted us to take a second look at the river route, where you are traveling a largely well-protected linear route with plenty of options for ducking out of foul weather.

In addition, Scott had just completed his music CD "Tiller Dreams" featuring several songs about America's Great Loop boat trip. Since we didn't want to store 1,000 CDs in our attic, it seemed like a good idea to get the show on the road and spread Scott's cruising music around in the locations where it was conceived.

As we wended our way from the cheerfully patriotic Joliet, Illinois town dock, to the muddy waters of Bobby's Fish Camp, fixed in a comfort zone from already having done it once before, we remembered how the trip had renewed our faith in the United States of America. This is a lovely country with a lot of heart. In Beardstown, Illinois, the downtown barber hung out his "back in 15 minutes" sign so he could run us to the store for block ice. In Columbus, Mississippi, the marina threw itself wholeheartedly into a scheme to throw a Green Bay Packer football tailgate party. At Fin's Marina in Sebastian, Florida, the harbormaster and fellow marina guests helped me add additional lines to secure *Chip Ahoy* in a bad blow, while Scott was off on a ship delivery from Jamaica to Fort Lauderdale. Throughout both Loops, the good deeds abounded among boaters, marinas, and townsfolk. That kind of reciprocal hospitality and willingness to share is what is really important in life; this is why we cruise, and it is also why we are at our most comfortable and relaxed state when living aboard. Many ask why people make this trip. We have to ask, why not?

We are lucky that our families and friends are generally supportive of what some consider a madcap caper. Many of our friends are boaters of one sort or another, so they don't consider us any weirder than usual. We've been living aboard a sailboat every summer for more than 10 years, so everyone is accustomed to Cyndi and Scott being "out somewhere." We consider it a rare blessing to be able to complete the Loop. We have seen heartbreaking situations where boaters have had to turn around due to health problems, family tragedies, or simply because they discovered the lifestyle wasn't at all what they'd imagined. On that darker side, I do think that some of our loved ones and acquaintances are left feeling a bit put out that we could be as self-centered, irresponsible, and irrational as to abandon the rat race and go gadding about on the water for months at a time.

Although it remained unspoken, clearly some people we are close to felt we were deserting them. They required a lot of reassurance. Luckily, in this day and age, it is possible to keep in touch and keep a handle on personal and business affairs when traveling on a boat. Cell phones, computers and a good mail-forwarding service, are essentials on our vessel.

It is also apparent to us that many landlubbers cannot grasp the beauty of travel at a slow pace. They are shocked to hear we may only travel 30-50 miles per day. Often, it is a relief to talk to fellow Loopers and other cruisers who "get" what we're doing, because they've done or are doing it themselves!

Contrary to those who envision the trip as an unabridged cocktail cruise, Looping is a lot of work. The continual learning curve expands the mind, body, and soul. Every aspect of our boating skills improved, from docking and anchoring, to negotiating around tow-barges and safely through shoaly inlets. These skills are translatable to life back on land, lending renewed confidence, balance, crisis management, and the ability to truly relax, which is actually quite difficult to achieve in this rushed world where instant gratification seems to rule all too often. Confronted with different environments and cultures, successful cruisers learn to literally go with the flow.

There is something humbling and freeing about realizing that each of us truly are just a mere drop in the bucket. In this world, we are no more or no less than the sum of nature. The Gulf of Mexico doesn't care if there is no cell phone reception. The dolphins aren't concerned about the stock market. The seagulls don't give a hoot that you haven't had a haircut in six months. The wind won't listen to your directions. The ocean waves will ebb and swell regardless of your schedule or desires. What's that old saying, "Time and tide wait for no man." My big takeaway from our two Loops is realizing that it isn't all about me. I can let go of the burden of believing that my problems and challenges are paramount.

More practically, our exposure to so many harbors and marinas has attuned us to what makes a good marina, and how to answer boater needs. Knowing what works and what isn't effective in marina operations has made all the difference in our latest endeavor: Scott has taken the helm of our local marina as Houghton County Harbormaster.

Early in our sailing life, I was fairly certain I'd need to buy one of those "Don't Yell" t-shirts. I am happy to report we are getting better at hand signals that don't involve the middle finger. Our underway skills often resemble those of a well-oiled team, and our 25-year marriage is stronger, happier, and more romantic thanks to cruising America's Great Loop. It was a privilege to have so much time alone with my husband. And when we needed time alone or in the companionship of others, there was always an opportunity for Scott to go talk engines/boat systems with someone, or for me to go to the bookstore, or shopping, or just do laundry with the "girls."

Scott and I have numerous and similar interests, but are both content to pursue our own hobbies. For example, I read and wrote voraciously, while he surfed the Internet. Having my own guitar player and singer aboard was quite pleasurable. There's nothing like a private concert in a remote bayou to warm your spirits and remind you how lucky you are!

My worst experience was a major rigging malfunction between Sebastian and Melbourne on the Florida ICW in late April. Gusting west winds broke the head stay, shredded the headsail, and sent the roller furling drum cannoning around the deck. Scott gathered the whipping mess, hanging off the port side a la Mary Poppins. We dropped anchor in the channel and wrestled the headsail down, screw by screw, feeding it down the heavy extrusions. At some point, a shackle smacked me in the forehead. There was a lot of blood, but no great harm done. The wound is just one of the lines on my forehead now! Although I sobbed after I got smacked, I wasn't scared for us, just annoyed by the expense and tension, and worried about the compromise to our rigging.

Luckily, Scott is an electronic technician and former cable guy, so he got 'er done with a heavy-duty cable TV clip that held the mast and rigging up until we could transit to St. Augustine for repairs. Later on in the Loop, I had the bejesus scared out of me on the Alligator River, during a fast-moving thunder and lightning storm. Since a strike is so random, I did figure that if our time was up, it was up. Scott, the more pragmatic of the two of us, trailed jumper cables off the stern, and we spent most of the storm discussing the path of least resistance. At least it distracted me from the bolts and rumbles! I only knew that he had been worried when he hailed Alligator River Marina. He immediately booked us for the night after we got through the bridge. Scott is a true passagemaker, but even he had had enough for one day.

The best experiences – and there were many – most always include wildlife encounters. Even on the toxic portions of the Illinois, where the signs warn against touching the water, the ungainly graacks of the herons startled and delighted us. We chuckled at wild turkeys trotting along the Tennessee-Tombigbee Waterway and mooed at wading cows. Snoozing gators, swimming deer, flipping leopard rays, cavorting dolphins, and snorting manatees populated our fabulous Loop menagerie. Surrounded by thousands of great white pelicans on the rivers, it felt as if we had stumbled into the midst of a National Geographic Special. We would see the white pelicans again near Cape Canaveral, where they mingled with exotic pink flamingos – a rare sight indeed that sent me rushing down below to mark it in the bird book. As Scott always says, "There is so much life in the water." The Loop provided a pleasing contrast to the stark crystal blue persuasion of Lake Superior's wide-open, largely unpopulated waters. When I ask Scott what his best experience was, he just says, "The whole thing."

Each sector of the Loop has its own charms... fall in Kentucky and Tennessee, especially the bays of the Land Between the Lakes; Halloween in Mississippi, when the yams and cotton are ready for harvest; Thanksgiving with the dolphins of Ingram Bayou, Alabama; Fresh oysters in Apalachicola, Florida, on our December 6, wedding anniversary; Christmas, New Year's and Epiphany in Tarpon Springs, Florida – these are just a few of my favorite areas. We tend to favor small towns with friendly people, and/ or remote anchorages with spectacular natural scenery. Experiencing the Trent-Severn Waterway for the first time on our second Loop served to show us that you could Loop your entire boating life and still discover treasures that are new to you. That's a truism along the entire route. The Carolinas and the Chesapeake in particular, still call to me. "Bew-fort" (Beaufort, South Carolina) and "Bo-fort" (Beaufort, North Carolina) are only a sampling; and we have yet to do the eastern shore of the Chessie. In the future, my cruising goal is to go out of the country to the Bahamas, Mexico, and perhaps Belize, and the Rio Dulce.

We will see. If I never get that brave or lucky, at least I feel at home in the waters of America's Great Loop.

Charlevoix, Michigan

For More Information on Cruising the

Great Loop

Visit the Favors' Popular Blog with Photography and
Stories of their Experiences while Doing the Loop.

www.favorsgreatloopblog.com
www.favorsweb.com

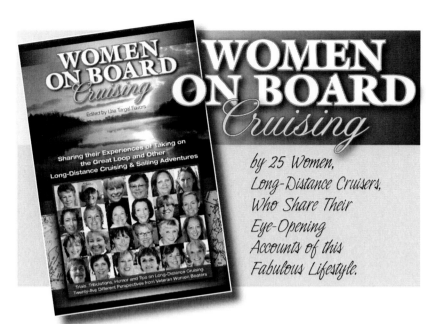

Using many different perspectives to tell of the trials and tribulations of long-distance cruising, 25 women share their unique experiences. This book offers the reader a chance to find out what might work for them under similar situations or they may just take comfort in the sharing and supportive accounts by this warm and amusing group of women who are each, seasoned, long-distance cruisers.

Collectively, they tried to show how this kind of lifestyle could be invigorating, rewarding and life changing. One of the things these 25 women have in common is the willingness to learn and take a risk at an unknown challenge sometimes for their partner or, more importantly, themselves. This is not a shy group; they have a lot to say.

You don't have to be a woman or even a boater to enjoy reading this book, every reader will enjoy the warmth, humor and resourcefulness that's shared within.

Questions! Doubts! You have so many before you set out! Well, just when you'd thought there was no one out there who understood you, along comes this awesome book, filled with warm women's voices offering clever advice, and helpful been-there-felt-that reassurance. It's like sitting down with a cup of tea and a support group of experienced fellow cruisers who can't wait to show you the ropes, and how cruising changed their lives and priorities.
– BERNADETTE BERNON, *BoatU.S. Magazine,* and *Cruising World*

Women On Board Cruising • Favors Ventures • 276 pages